SEVEN LIVES
AUTOBIOGRAPHY

SEVEN LIVES

AUTOBIOGRAPHY

SIR HARI SINGH GOUR

GYAN

Published by

Gyan Publishing House
5, Ansari Road
Daryaganj, New Delhi-110002
Phone: 011-47034999, 9811692060
E-mail: books@gyanbooks.com

Distribution Network
gyanbooks.com
India, USA, Canada, UK, Australia

ISBN: 978-93-6920-693-3 (PB)

First Published, 1924

2nd Impression 2025

Printed at: Gyan Press, Delhi.

SEVEN LIVES AUTOBIOGRAPHY
Author: SIR HARI SINGH GOUR

'SEVEN - LIVES'

AUTOBIOGRAPHY

OF DR. SIR H. S. GOUR
& OTHER ALLIED PIECES

The autobiography was begun on some date in 1942 and finished on 23 January, '44.

Ah tell me not thou sage and bard divin
That glory like the man will pass away,
And beauty like a flower only shine
And blush awhile — poor creature of a day;
Nay, flowers full many have I often seen,
That seem'd bespread on heaths a paradise
O'er which the ever wild wind hath not been
But stay'd and linger'd long for warm surprise,
Nor e'en fell winter lack'd a passing tear
But dew'd the bank whereon the flowers grew,
And though they dead, their fragrance still lives there
And gives through every spot the sweetest view—
Through fields, and stars, and snow with bare-armed tree,
Nay, beauty never dies, but lives eternally.

H. S. GOUR
in his 'RANDOM RHYMES'

SEVEN LIVES

Introduction

THIS is my second attempt about 18 months after the first draft of my autography was destroyed by enemy action. Like one's dead children it was the best I had even penned, and its destruction left me with a sore memory of the time spent on my literary exertion, but now that after long last I have ventured to recomplete my biography, I think it is only fair to me, and I trust to the reader, that I should reveal my inward thoughts on this composition.

In my life I have read many biographies including autobiographies, and while I have found all of them interesting, personal and pleasant, I have found some of them too personal and not as detached as I should expect a biography, even if it is an autography to be. I have been told that many biographies are in their essence mere camouflaged autographies, since no biographer can compose a fair and full record of a life without consulting the biographee who supplied from his memory or out of his papers the facts that make his biography full and readable. But though it is so, I will concede that whether it is so or not, no biography is worth its name unless it is strictly truthful and faithfully imparts to the reader the lessons of one's acts and omissions from which he might profit. By reading many biographies for this purpose in my teens when I was still at school, I found that most of them illustrated in their own way the grand truth that Lord Chesterfield imparted in his published letters to his son that if you wish to get on in this world, then avoid doing what you think is right, but do what would be pleasing to your fellow-men. As I have all expatiated on this subject later on I shall not enlarge it here, beyond stating that as I have not got on in the world according to the views of the world, It has not been because I did not know which was the royal road to success, but I deliberately chose the path of Truth and avoided the opportunism. My life will not therefore interest those who wish to get on in life, except by telling them and emphasising for them that the route to olympus is diagonally opposite to that for Veritas if there be such a thing for the practice of Verity and nothing different or nothing else.

Some of the biographies I have read became interesting because they were racy and anecdotal and so amused the reader who naturally prizes what he is amused with. My life has been quite varied and has taken me to Olympus though I have merely sojourned there for a time in circumstances which have merged my identity with its legitimate denizens, though I have remained distruct from them and have in fact avoided them, not secretly but openly as will be apparent to those who made through the ensuing pages of this composition.

As such my life may interest those few who like myself view the world and all its belongings with contempt wondering how we the singular and unique accident of nature and the universe lack the premordial sense of yet not having been able to set our house in order, and how in all its essence our life is even less secure than that of the wild beast or bird which seems to have fixed upon a better scheme of Live and Let Live than this glorious product of the Universe who passes his whole life in misery and want bereft of peace or happiness that he can count on as his earthly heritage.

But I am afraid I am revealing myself too early to my reader. For this chapter is not the omega but the Alpha of my career, and I intend to indite the first impressions that has made this work possible.

But as it is I have already let out two arcanes prematurely. Let me resume my introduction. In my view, before a person starts to indite the story of one's life one has to make up his ideal. The first is—has he anything to say? If his life has followed the conventional track of the million who live and die, there is nothing special to say. That has not been my life. If not, has that departure been merely freakish or designed for a purpose ? I know I have shaped my life so. That was one reason why I have made premature disclosure of two of the points here. But there remain others of which I must refer. Should the Life be a didactic sermon in detail or a flowing narrative with no eye on the Decalogue ? It may instruct, guide and illustrate a life passed out of the ordinary and its ups and downs, mostly downs, which might derive as a lesson to 400 millions of human being living under another rule and which upsets all normal conceptions of life, its hopes and ambitions, its possibilities and urges, its adaptability to its enviornments, normal and abnormal, all presenting a picture more entertaining than a novel, more sensational because of its back-ground of reality, more chastening and in the end more spiritualizing to mankind.

Many biographies are penned for the direct interest of one's family and friends. As will be apparent from the sequel I have only a handful of the first in no way interested in my strife and struggles and still fewer of the second who are likely to feel interested in the subject to care to make through its pages. One common feature that these pages possess with many biographies is the world-wide range of their author and his acquaintance with most of the men who have occupied or now occupy the centre of the stage. It seems to me that alone makes this work necessary, as I wish my countrymen to realise the polar difference between the diplomatic platitudes and the real feelings that divide the acts and utterances of many men whom luck has pitched into the saddle of power in the most cr tical period of human history. That being decisive the questions that aroused my thoughts were (1) How long should the work be and (2) what should be its title ? As to the first I have collected materials to compose a work ten times the present volume, but by severe clipping and condensation I have been able to reduce it to the size of an ordinary fiction. But in doing so I had necessarily to omit numerous minor incidents which though important have since been forgotten, though they have not failed to have their trail on later events to which I have referred. The work has thus ceased to be a dairy but still remains a sketch. What then should I call it ? I have read many books, extremely interesting, but published under impossible pseudonyms—such is the readable autobiography of a man belonging to my own profession, Augustins Birrell, who acknowledges to have selected the title of his life "Things past Redress" from Shakespeare. How he could have descended upon it I donot know for there are many things past redress, but certainly not one's life however wicked. Other books called "My Autobiography", "My Life," "My Struggles" are more direct but too bald to attract a reader and many a book owe their popularity to a happy title. Such was Marie Corrélle's "Sorrows of Satan", a work which offended as much against the rules of taste as of idiom and grammar but of which many million copies were sold and which was filmed and became the common talk of every drawing-room in the Victorian days when I was reading at Cambridge. And there are other books that have sold because of their lucky title. I have selected the title to convey to the reader the object I have had in compiling my Life—Its lessons prefigure its main purpose. Let me add that an autobiography suffers from the suspicion of egotistical bombast, an apotheosis of self-laudation and a self-seeking advertisement. As I am nearing my eightieth year I must be deemed to have outlived most of these vanities that haunt men and that at one time haunted me. I am now like one writing from the grave and my life may then be taken as a sober narrative with no cut flowers to decorate it.

CHAPTER 1

MY ANCESTRY AND EARLY LIFE

NO life is complete without a knowledge of its ancestry, the more so in the modern stage of biological research when many of man's qualities, good and bad, are directly traceable and indeed traced to his ancestors.

So far as I am concerned I can summarise my ancestry both on the paternal and maternal side in due words that they were all farmers living in the villages adjoining Saugor to which my grandfather Thakur Man Singh shifted and where my father Thakur Thakht Singh was born and so were all his children, 3 sons and 2 daughters, of whom I happen to be the youngest. Adhar Singh, my eldest brother, was really the second son of my father as Onkar Singh, his first son, died early and Adhar was to all intents and purposes his eldest son. My father had married my mother Ladli Bai who was the second sister of a family who tilled land in the village Semar Kheda. Her elder sister married an officer in the service of a Bundela Chief and when I was aged 5, I remember her daughter, a very pretty girl, playing with me and by accident dropping me on a stone which gave me a nasty cut on my right eyebrow the scar of which has remained as it were my permanent birth-mark.

I have a distinct recollection of this girl and of his father who came on a short visit to my mother. All the members of my mother's family were fair and would pass for a European being tall and white-skinned as are the many families of Bundela Rajputs who have for generations settled in the highlands of BundelKhand. My mother was nick-named "Bhuri" or the "White" because she was blonde with golden hair and blue eyes which she passed on to her two daughters and her eldest son. My father was short, square-set and swarthy and I happen to be a cross being wheat-coloured, short and square-set. My intermediate brother Ganpat Singh was even darker than me, but he was tall and well-built. I am not good at guessing height but I think my father was 5'-5", my mother the same if not an inch or two taller while Adhar could not be less than 5'-9". He was accounted a tall, fair man—Fair he certainly was as he was often taken for a European. His hair had turned prematurely grey but his eyes were light-brown and his face had become pitted with the marks of smallpox, otherwise he was *beau ideal* of the fair. My two sisters Lilawati and Mohan Bai were both white and possessed a figure which may be truly described as ideal. They had very light brown hair and sparkling eyes. They were both very clever while my younger sister had very early developed a flair for mathematics, a subject which was dear to my mother who though illiterate had invented a practical mathematics of her own which she used to solve many intricate problems. She had a mathematical precision in her words and talk and a phenominal memory which I am said to have inherited. My younger sister went to school and carried off all its prizes but my other sister had no schooling inspite of which she was sparking in her wit and talk. That a high vein of intelligence ran in the family will be evident from the fact that my brother Adhar was put to school at the usual age of 5 and passed in the first division the Matriculation Examination of Calcutta University—It was in 1860 ten years before I was born. My mother was said to have a septennial crop and all her children were divided by that age with the result that my eldest brother was many years senior to me and I cannot recall his figure otherwise than as a grey-bearded old man, older in fact to look at than my own father who though grey wore his age well. In the sixties Saugor had no facilities for higher education. Its Government High School was then as it is still a secondary school.

Like the *alumini* of an English public School those of the High School were instinctively drawn to form an academic family pledged to social service and comradeship for the rest of their lives. Balmukund Shukul Ram Krishna Shrikhande, Gajadhar Shukul and my brother thus became the quartette who passed their lives in closest friendship. My brother had matriculated quite young, but lacking the means to

Dr. Gour at the age of 14

Dr. Gour's ancestral house at Sanechari Tori, Sagour (The house where he was born)

prosecute his collegiate studies at Agra, the nearest place with a college, he entered service as did the other three and of them my brother realised his youthful ambition of taking a degree which he did in 1880 when he was well over 50 and on the verge of retirement from Government service in which he rose to be the equivalent of a District Judge. Ramkrishna ran *proxima accetit*; while Balmukund Purohit who had joined the Educational administration retired as an Inspector. Gajadhar had a more versatile future. He became an accountant in the Executive Engineer's Office which he left and after some years of idleness he was taken on in the service of Travancore State from where he returned to end his days in unwanted retirement.

As for my brother he joined a clerical post in th district office from where he was promoted to be a Tehsildar of Dhamtari on a salary of Rs. 150/- and thence he fought his way, unaided by any except his integrity in days when it was exceptional industry and assiduity to be the clerk of Court, in the Divisional Commissioner's office at Raipur on a salary of Rs. 200/- P. M., later promoted to be the Deputy Registrar of the Judicial Commissioner's Court on Rs. 250/- and then as an E. A. C. which was the peak and pinnacle of a Native's ambition in those days when all higher jobs were earmarked for a European. My brother was the sole bread-winner of our family. As my father passed his long life doing nothing and lived on a monthly allowance my brother made him first Rs. 50/-, then Rs. 30/- and later Rs. 10/-. This progressive reduction was partially due to his own quickening ambition to do what his parental poverty had debarred him from doing, namely to complete his education. My brother was very fond of books and had collected about 500 even when he was a clerk. His ambition to take a degree and outturn his fellows made him extremely frugal with his own expenses and out of his pittance he saved as much as he possibly could to enable him to take a degree and get called to the Bar for which he proceeded to Cambridge in 1881, then aged about 50, and after 3 years of intensive study took its degree in Law with honours and was placed in the second division of the Law Tripos, which was a unique distinction for one who had spent his while life in clerical service. He was called to the Bar about the same time. So equipped he returned to rejoin his subordinate post of an E.A.C. in which he had hoped a rise on account of his unique qualities, but he found the Government indifferent. On the other hand, taking advantage of his new qualifications they posted him to a highly litigious district where he started clearing up years of accumulated arrears, but with no gain to himself. The Chief Commissioner of the Province was a wily Scot, Alexander Mackenzie, who ignored his academic laurels and gave him Hoshangabad because its judicial work needed a Judge who would be able to combine disposal with despatch. My brother did both, though his method did not please the Bar who had grown rich on procrastination and adiournments.

After long years spent in intensive application to his exacting duties my brother was overcome by *ennui* and disappointment. He felt that ability and integrity was no passport to promotion and so while he had earned pension, he committed the folly of throwing up his billet and joined the Bar of the very district in which he had filled the Bench. He got on well, but his advancing years and strenuous toil began to tell on him. In 1893 he got a mild dose of paralysis and he shifted to his native place, Saugor, where he rebuilt our family-home in which he passed away in 1915.

So far as my father is concerned I was born when he was my brother's pensioner. My mother told me that, in his earlier years he had taken a job in the Police, as Chief Constable, now corresponding to a Sub-Inspector, but as soon as my brother got employed he found living on him more aggreeable, and though my mother had goaded him to do something to kill time if not to earn an honest penny, my father turned a deaf ear to her threats and entreaties, though at one time he was half-heartedly inclined to turn to agriculture and purchased 35 acres of absolute occupancy land in Deol Chauri, a village 30 miles from Saugor, but which he left his remote casteman to till for him. I remember this gentleman who used to bring a few sheaves of green grain from our field in January or February every year which is all the harvest we enjoiued from our field which was said to be rich and fertile with a well of its own for its irrigation.

But my father, as his father before him, detested country life with no company and no school to educate his children. Nor had he any incentive to make the change. My grandfather had built a house in the Sanicheri Tori of Saugor which my father extended and rebuilt and all his children were born in this house in which my younger sister, Mohan, my mother and my brother also died. It was on the whole a lucky house to which with all the vicissitudes of our lives my mother clung as its sole occupant, when I was in Europe studying, and my father was at Jabalpur looking after my brother's children who had been left in direct charge of Mr. Vishnu Panth Shrikhande, elder brother Ramkrishna, my brother's class-mate. This gentleman was schoolmaster in the local Normal School and drew a salary of Rs. 30/-. He was a careful, well-balanced man and lived extremely well on his small salary. He rented a house a few doors away at Gadha Phatak—i. e. on the road to the village Gadha, on Rs. 15/- P.M. and we all lived there in 1882-83 when my brother was a student at Cambridge. My father died there in 1883, aged over 80 but I am unable to give his exact age; but my mother told me that both her and our families were long-lived, as Man Singh had died in his eighties and a legend about his death was vouched for by my mother who was then a girl of 12 and had just come into our house hold after her marriage. She said that Man Singh had for years lived upon nothing save a small rental of his farm which he had sublet. One morning he had an early bath and at about 8 he emerged from his room into the verandah, fully dressed in white with his sword dangling by his side as if he were going to a battle, called all the house-mates including my two parents and told them that his hour was near. He spoke farewell to his people and then, sword in hand, lay down on the carpet where he died. My mother told me that my grand-father was both in appearance and mentality like my father, easy-going, lazy with no ambition and no drive, no enemies and no friends, no kinsmen or relations and such was my father's life from the day of my birth to that of his death.

His daily routine was as follows. He woke up at 6 in the morning and after adjusting his toilette he used to eat or drink water if he got nothing else which had become his daily routine under the stern discipleship of my mother. At about 1 A. M. he used to go the tank to have a bath and returning he would spend half an hour on his "Puja" i.e. worship of three or four brazen idols and a stone-egg the phallic symbol of the God Shiva. He used to take his mid-day meal cooked by my mother or sister and later on by my brother Ganpat Singh's wife and then fall into his *siesta* from which he roused himself at about 2, when he washed and dressed and went down the hill to a bearded barber's den in the spacious compound of which the two played *Chausar* till 6 when he returned home to take his supper and go to bed.

My mother's life was a contrast to his. She was always up and doing and when she found that the family-allowance had been reduced, she purchased a Charkha (spinning-wheel) and started spinning cotton in which she was engaged from 1 to 7 or 8 P. M. After her 3 days' toil she sold her yarn and purchased cotton-wicks for making fresh yarn. She made about 4 or 5 annas out of the sale which she employed in buying household necessities. I was ten when I was the recipient of a small scholarship founded to commemorate the connection of one Mitchel as the First Headmaster of the Saugor school. Its value was Rupees two a month and the Headmaster Mr. Kirpa Shankar Jha, a man much attached to his students to whom he extended his paternal care, insisted that I should attend a night-class for study which I had to do but which was sheer waste of time as these classes were crowded and consisting as they did of students from different classes there was no unity of study or attention. Later on I was permitted to study alone in the house of one Laxmi Narain, a teacher—not mine, who sat as uncomfortably to watch over me as I sat to study under him. But I was proud of my scholarship and entreated my mother to stop her wheel and take from my scholarship the money she made there on. But she could not stay idle and often told me that if she did not spin, she would grind which would be more irksome to her and distressing to me. So we arranged a truce till I passed my Middle school examination in 1881 and was awarded a scholarship which enabled me to proceed to Jabalpur to prosecute my further studies. My younger sister and my playmate, then aged 9 or 10, carried my luggage-bag to a point where it was put into a camel-cart with myself for Kareli, a Railway station

75 miles from Saugor, which was the only point of approach by Railway to Jabalpur. The fare from Saugor to Kareli was Rs. 2 and the Camel-Cart took 2 nights and day to reach it.

I was then aged 15, so that the difference in age between me and my sister was only 5 years and this is the last look I had of that angel clad in coarse Khaddar, for we could not then afford finer cloth. She said nothing as we parted but my heart stopped beating as she turned her back, never again to see me for she was carried off by the epidemic of Cholera in 1889 while I was at Cambridge. And if I ever dream of a hereafter, it is to meet her again and when I find myself surrounded by apulence and affluence I do not feel happy but sad that she is not there to enjoy it. I am writing this in 1942, more than 60 years after her death, but her picture is still vivid before my eyes, and the one consolation I shall feel in my death is that I might meet her again. I penned a sonnet and published it in my volume of verse published by Simpkim Marshall which the press acclaimed as very touching. May I subjoin it ?

(SONNET)

IN MEMORIAM

Nay, thou'rt not dead ; thy fairy-form still shines
In bowers, where lilies and chaste daisies bloom,
The winds that dance a minuet with the pines,
And woo into soft smiles the Even gloom.
The full moon liveried in her argent light,
The stars in holy raptures tremulous beam,
The sweets of hope, affectionate beauties' sight,
And love's fond kisses, youthful fancy's dream.
Nay, sights of woe, in silence eloquent,
And all where joy or dismal sorrow reigns,
Thy soul, like voice of thrilling music sent
Through hills and vales, her presence still proclaims :
For soul to soul, her kindred element,
And body till bespirited her soil claims.

My sister was not merely my pal but my mascot and when I left India for England I am sorry to say that I had to go from Hoshangabad direct to the boat in Bombay and had no money to pay farewell visit to my dear mother. My two sisters had by then got married, the elder one was married to a cosharer at Mohari, a village about 30 miles north of Saugor on the Saugor-Lalitpur Road. My younger sister, Mohan, was married to a similar cosharer at Chil Pahdi about 3 miles off the Tehsil town of Banda on this road. My brother Adhar Singh was married while young to the daughter of a tenant of M. Tatarwada not far from Mohari. She was illiterate and good enough for the usual household duties of cooking and housekeeping.

My other brother Ganpat Singh who was a failure in life was married to a girl from a village, also illiterate and orthodox. He passed no examination but was appointed a Famine Naib Tahsildar for a while, after which he became a clerk in the Court of Wards in which he stagnated till an epidemic overtook him and he died leaving a widow and some children whom I supported till they too got absorbed in the clerical line of a district office. My elder sister Lilawati was married by my father to an orthdox family in Mohari. She has some children who follow the wake of their rustic farmers. She came to see me after my return to join the Indian Bar at Raipur but a few years after she contracted a spleen complaint which carried her off leaving me alone to plough my lonely furrow in a lonely world.

Upon my return to India in 1892 I was qualified for call to the Bar, but was not called as I lacked the £100 I needed to pay the fee. As my nephew Murli Manohar Singh was still in England and could not pass the Bar Examination for which my brother Adhar Singh had sent him with me, he ascribed his ill-success to my negligence in supervising his studies, which was not true. He was only 3 years' younger and had really no brains nor application, but his detention created a coolness between me and my brother who left me to devise my own future, which I did by sending my book of poems to the then Chief Commissioner of the Central Provinces Sir Antony Macdonell—who afterwards became Lord Macdonell on his retirement from the Indian Civil Service and made a mark as under-Secretary of state for Ireland.

He sent for me, appointed me an E.A.C., a rare departure from the routine of the day when this appointment was reserved for the rankers as a prize for those who had made a mark in the subordinate posts. It created a sensation in the Province, the more so as the Chief had created a vacancy to put me in, as will be more fully described in a later chapter.

I have now finished describing all I know about my relations. My brother Adhar and myself were never very friendly on my return to India. Years or so after me his son Murli Manohar returned after his call to the Bar, but with no degree. He joined his father at Hoshangabad and started his practice under him. In the May of 1893 when the courts were closed he used to go out visiting his friends with whom he used to play Bridge. May is one of the hottest months of summar, and Murli's mother who cooked for the family used to savour her *Dal* with tamarind juice. As all her utensils were made of brass or Pewter she stored for her son his rice and *dal* in a pewter vessel and as Murli returned late to take his dinner the *dal* he ate had become sceptic and at midnight he felt the effect of sceptic poisoning which inspite of best medical aid, carried him off. Naturally this gave a rude hock to my brother who had built all his hopes on his son.

He had four other sons, but of these the second had predeceased Murli and the rest were unable to do anything at school, with the result that the death of Murli, the last and the only hope of my brother, broke my brother's stoic heart and as I had by then started my practice in Bhandara from where my professional reputation took me to several adjoining districts my brother became more openly estranged from me and though I did all I could to appease him he was infact never appeased. As I had very heavy professional work from the very start, it was not before a couple of months after his death that I was able to pay my brother a condolence visit which assuaged him for the time being and he told me to take away his Library as he had no further use for it. I had then decided to compose my work on the Law of Transfer for which my brother's library came in handy. So I removed it and at the same time to Raipur when the Zamindar of Fingeshwar had engaged me to conduct an important case involving the impartible nature of his Zamindari.

Murli had been married on his return to an illiterate rustic girl of our caste and he was otherwise inclined to be orthodox in his thought and ways. But as it was he died within two years of his return home and left a blank in his family which was never filled up. It cast a gloom of perpetual melancholy on my brother and though he bravely carried on and was to all appearance cheerful and happy, the premature death of his eldest son had wounded his heart which during the 22 years that he outlived his son never failed to corrode it.

As both my brother and myself had broken away from routine occupation of our caste and family, we were both in fact ignored if not outcasted by the few remote relations we could call our own. Like the Kshatriyas generally the few relations we had were all resident in small villages; they were illiterate and ignorant and too orthodox to tolerate or acknowledge a kinsman who had crossed the black water and on the return had made no pretence of expiation.

In the 'nineties of the last century foreign travel was still a deadly sin and its non-expiation an offence visited by the direst contempt and ostracism of the hegemony. We had no organised panchayat to appeal to and there was no set body to try up for our transgressions, the result being that we were damned without trial by the fanatical floating opinion of the tribe.

As my business lay in the eastern half of the Province, where there were few Rajputs and these had a regiment of their own and were strangers to the Rajputs of Saugor, whom they would treat as much their kinsmen as the inhabitants of Timbuctoo. The sympathies of a race widen with education, but the Kshatriyas of the east were as illiterate as the Kshatriyas of Bundelkhand with whom they recognise no consanguinous affinity, the more so because living as they have for ages in the midst of aborogines with whom they have much in common—their dialect and tradition—they have deteriorated into a distinct sub-caste which feel towards Kshatriyas of the north as much comradic as the Kshatriyas of the North feel towards them.

And both of them taboo one of them who has crossed the sea and so forfeited his orthodoxy. That apart the Kshatriyas throughout India still remain uneducated, ignorant and superstitious, following today as they have been doing since ages past a narrow line of life dominated only by tradition of which a loose caste opinion is the final interpreter.

As such my brother Adhar was a life-long outcast since his return from Europe and as had I had lived and dined with him even before I went to Europe, my sister, for the sake of her own safety, ceased to dine with us and she cooked her own food, unpolluted by my sister-in-law's utensils and presence. It is scarcely necessary to add that in our professional and public life we were all alone and received no assistance of any kind, direct or indirect, in any measure from the socially down-trodden members of our community who are mostly darwans or sepoys unless they be princes whose mentality is by no means different.

Whatever success each of us secured in life must, therefore, be ascribed to our own individual effort unaided by any one because of our nationality, provincial, local or tribal support. On the other hand, we had to fight the strong handicap from which we suffered, because we were after all mere "natives" and had neither the prestige or glamour of a whiteman who was much sought after because all the higher judiciary was white, drawn from the civil service whose members' knowledge of law, judicial procedure and policy was individualistic and personal, which gave the white Barristar an advantage due to his social contact with that class, wholly denied to the native. It must be within the recollection of many of my confreres how thoroughly incompetent white Barrister made a fortune out of such official patronage.

My brother's practice at the Bar of Hoshangabad suffered by his having to face such uneven competition from such outside counsel. But during his stay at Hoshangabad he got on well, though not too well because of his temper which antagonised both the Bench and the Bar. He would often lapse into a fallacious argument and would support it tooth and claw even though futility was obvious. And he would hurl at the Court a plethora of cases and texts drawn from his copious library, till he relieved himself of it on his son's death. On his shifting to Saugor my brother's age and growing infirmity allied to the fact that Saugor is poor in litigation made a noticeable decline in his pratice which dwindled into insignificance, so that when he died he did not leave a heavy banking account, though what little he had left was soon squandered by his sons.

I have now given sufficient account of the members of my family from which it will be obvious that my parents had left me nothing being themselves life-long pensioners of my brother, and all I inherited from them was a healthy constitution, and I believe the brain that made a mark in my brother's life and mine came mostly out of our mother's blood, and so did my brother's temper since my brother was more like my mother—fair, tall, well-built and temperamental. As for myself I appear to be a blend more like the father in outward appearance and like the mother in the output of energy. I am also temperamental but, knowing as I do, I keep it under control and have never offended or quarreled with anybody, though I have often to face maniacs and intemperate loafers who retail to their friends their proud achievement of having publicly insulted a well-known man.

As I am now a grandfather of children whose behaviour and pecadillos I have watched I am able to assert that there is more in heredity than psychologist gives credit for.

Late Dr Adhar Singh Gour when Tehsildar, C. P.

Late Dr Adhar Singh Gour when E. A C., C. P.

Late Dr. Adhar Singh Gour, Bar-at-Law

Late Dr. Murlimanohar Singh Gour, Bar-at-Law, eldest son of Dr. Adhar Singh Gour

An early portrait of Dr. Harisingh Gour

CHAPTER II

MY CHILDHOOD

IN this chapter I wish to recount some incidents of my childhood from the age of 5 to 15 when I passed my Middle School examination which entitled me to join an Intermediate College for my matriculation. That College had been shifted from Saugor to Jabalpur in the seventies and with it Saugor lost her academic jewel and it paved the way for its growing decadence into an insignificant town of no importance which it is today.

But there was a time when Saugor was the headquarters of a Commissioner who ruled over the "Saugor and Narbudda territories". Saugor had a mint and a Euro ean garrison, besides Indian cavalry and infantry. It was what Ja alpur is now, a brigade headquarters. Its population then must have been much larger for it is now 50,000.

Saugor is built on a spur of a Vindhya plateau upon hich stand Bhopal, Indore and Mhow and is 2,000 feet above the sea-level. It is hot in summer but not so hot as Nagpur, while its winter is cold needing fires, which are necessary for comfort for three or four months (November to February). But even in the hottest period of the years (Say May upto the fall of rains in June) the nig s are cool and pleasant to sleep in the open air. The people of Saugor are mostly Hindus belonging to all castes. The fact is that Saugor was before 1863 a district attached to the Agra Province, transferred to the newly formed Central Provinces for administrative purposes. Consequently its people are to this day as of the United Provinces, and so are those of the whole Jabalpur division except Mandla the people of which are Gonds.

Saugor is so called because it is built round a large lake covering 300 acre of its soil. It was at one time a deep circular sheet of water around which the town was built on low hills from which a fine view of the water was available. For sheer scenic splendour Saugor stands unique, but as it has nothing to enrich it, it remains resigned to the small population who live by marketing their farm-produce to which an unwelcome addition is made in the slaughter houses opened to export dry beef to Burma. But of all places In the Central Provinces Saugor is the only place where the farm produce is as varied as it is of the highest quality. It is a prolific field for potatoes and pea-nuts, while its lentils are rich in vitamins drawn from its black cotton soil, where however cotton does not flourish because it has a copious rainfall some 45 inches against 30, beyond which cotton will not grow.

I do not know what had attracted my grandfather from Chil pahadi where he was said to have had a farm and I donot know why with transfer to Saugor he did not give more than a modium of vernacular education to my father. It might have been the question of ways and means. But as his death-bed scene proves it he was a soldier at heart and died a soldier with his sword beside him. His thoughts did not run in any other channel. He was like many Kshatriyas I have met, more proud of his blood than cared to work for a better living. And so he lived and died poor—"a penny-less laid with a long pedigree".

So far as I am concerned I have a clear recollection of my father following his daily routine from the age of five when I was put into a *Pathashala* run by a neighbour who taught me the multiplication and tables and the Hindi alphabet. I was one of the twenties, all of whom did not go very far, though we all started life with equal enthusiasm. Two years later I was enlisted in the Hindi Branch school at Katra below the hill on which we lived. A Mr. Madan Lal was our master. He was a full six-footer Kayasth who used to heighten his figure by tying a lengthy white pugree. And as he lived some 100 yards behind the school he had built up a tradition that his devout pupils should escort him from his house. I joined the 10 or 12 of them who did this every day. He had the habit of pinching in the groins while his escort were spared. I did not take kindly to his mechanical lessons which merely loaded the memory without enriching the brain. But I carried on for 3 years after which we were promoted to the Zila school, which was regarded as a feather in our cap. While I was under his tutelage I remember his paying a visit to my father to congr tulate him upon my quick promotion. He said, "your son is like a spark (*tilga*) and he will shine like one". This remark made me very conceited and I was eager to meet my school-mates to whom I blurted out Madan Lal's compliment. It fired them with jealousy and most of them retorted that it was my own make up. They then nick-named me the 'spark" and I was sorry that I had told them what I did in my childish vanity.

The boys in my class-room were every months rated according to their "Number", that is merit, and as these numbers were given by moving the pupil from the bottom seat in the class to the top it was a great incentive to prepare our lessons and answer all questions correctly, otherwise we ran the risk of losing our number. I easily gained the top in a few days and retained it against all comers. My master treated me as the prize-boy of the class and when Mr. Kripa Shankar Jha, Head Master of the school, held our examination he found me so well qualified as to give me double promotion which was a rare compliment in the school. After this my sobriquet "Spark" was shorn of its irony and at the end of another year I was again selected for a similar promotion. I reached the fourth class in only two instead of four years.

As I was still at the top of my form I easily won the "Mitchel" scholarship of two rupees a month to which I have already referred. From my childhood I had taken a fancy to the collection of books of which I formed my library. I was fond of reading Readers of class above mine, which gave me the reputation of precocity and endeared me to my headmaster, whose anticipation was realized as I passed the Middle school examination in the the First class and obtained a Government scholarship for two years, but my ambition of topping the list was not gratified as that honour fell to one Mr. Debi Prasad Shrivastava and even the second place was taken by Mr. Prem Narain, of both of whom I shall speak later on.

It ended my studies at Saugor and with my scholarship I went to the Government High School at Jabalpur. I was then a short, slightly built stripling of 12. and on my arrival at Jabalpur. I naturally became a boarder as I knew no one in that large town, double the size of my Saugor, who would extend his hospitality to me, though a year later I found that my brother's schoolmate Mr. Gajadhar Shukla was there and on my paying him a visit he invited me to take my evening meals with his family, which I started doing but found the distance prohibitive and so resumed the usual routine of taking my meals at the Government Hostel run by the senior students. That course of life was quite new to me, but though I cried bitterly that I had been cut off from my home, my mother and my dear sister who cooked and fed me, I became soon reconciled to my forlorn life from which three senior students to whom I was billeted did everything to retrieve me.

They were kindly, helpful and played the parental part of giving me consolation and assistance. They were all Maratha Brahmins but caste and language did not abate their higher call of humanity. My father used to wear a golden ring and I wanted to emulate his example by wearing a similar ring which I got made out of the savings of my scholarship. This I sported at school and though it might be vulgar it excited the cupidity of a Saugor boy, son of a *Kachi* who had come to prosecute his studies in the company of his mother, who invited me once or twice to a meal. Though it was strictly against the caste-rule, the woman convinced me that as yet my thread-ceremony had not been performed I was free to dine with her which I did. She then induced me to shift to her room and I did so with all my belongings enclosed in a Khaddar bag which was secured with a one-anna padlock.

I used to take off my gold ring and deposit it into this bag at night, as I was afraid that some one might pinch it off my person while I was asleep. I think this was the *quasi*-parental advice given to me by the Kachi woman, who had laid designs on my ring and plotted with her son to secure it which she did the very first night I put it into the bag.

The next morning I was disconsolate and proceeded to Mr. Gajadhar Shukla's to complain. Mr. Shukla knew Mr. Lima, a Goan Police city Superintendent, who ordered an inquiry which led to the prosecution of the woman. The case was tried by a Mr. A. C. Duff,

I.C.S., since dead. He examined me and sentenced the woman to 4 months' imprisonment.

This was my first appearance in Court at the age of 13. The worry this case caused to me and the time it took made me neglect my studies with the result that I failed in the ensuing Matriculation Examination and with it stopped my scholarship, and as my father's allowance had by then already been reduced to Rs. 10/- P. M. it left no margin for my studies which I had to abandon and return to Saugor. The "Spark" reduced to a cinder. I was then 14 and in build and appearance slight, but I had no alternative but to look out for a job in the district Court or elsewhere, and the next 2 years I spent haunting every office with my application for a job which I failed to secure. One of my classmates, Raja Ram by name who had passed the Matriculation Examination in which I had failed became my job-hunting companion and I remember our applications to D. Wallace, Executive Engineer. He offered to Raja Ram a billet as coollies' mate on Rs. 10/- P.M. and to me on Rs. 6/- and both of us had to go to a roadside village 35 miles from Saugor. Raja Ram went but I did not as I resented the discrimination in pay made on the basis of our scholastic attainments.

However a few weeks later I managed to secure the billet of a Mess clerk on Rs. 20/- P.M. and I entered upon my duties with a show of my importance to my mother who curled her lips in doubt whether I would be able to keep it—as the clerk had to work from 9 A.M. to close on midnight. She was right. After a fortnight I fell ill and had to resign my post. I did not know what to do, how to employ my time and earn my daily bread. The only course open to me was to use the Rs. 10/- I had made in my train-fare to Nagpur where my brother was then posted as Deputy Registrar of the Judicial Commissioner's Court.

My brother received me coldly but advised me to continue my studies and pass the Matriculation examination. It was the soundest advice I ever had and in the result I not only passed that examination in the first division but headed the provincial list for which a cash-prize of Rs. 50/- was received, as also another prize, the Khaihrashwar prize of a silver watch and a scholarship of Rs. 20/- P.M. which made me quite independent of my brother who had in the meantime taken leave and left for his study at Cambridge. Fortunately for me I had also secured a special prize for mathematics which drew me to Mr. Bhagirath Prasad, professor of Mathematics in the Free Church Institution, later raised to a first-class college bearing the name of Mr. Hislop who was the First Missionary of that College at Nagpur and drowned on horse-back in the flooded Wardha river which he had crossed to conduct his geological researches which he embodied in a brochure on the subject named the "Geology of Nagpur".

My brother had taken two years' furlough and on his return he found that I had equally well passed the Intermediate Examination and carried off all the prizes—including the one given by my professor of Sanskrit to a student who secured the highest number of marks in "the Languages". His favourite pupil was a Maratha Brahmin Mr. Prabhakar Watak whose proficiency in Sanskrit was marvellous. I was very poor in that language and had studied what little I knew by rote. Now the maximum marks in those days were 200 in English and 100 in Sanskrit, or any other classical Vernacular. In the final result I had secured 140 marks and Mr. Watak 130. The prize of Rs. 50/- was therefore awarded to me, but not without overruling the donor's objection that being a professor of Sanskrit he had intended to offer the prize to one who obtained maximum marks in Sanskrit, which is what he had meant by the term "languages".

I also carried off Mr. Bhagirath Prasad's prize of a similar sum for similar proficiency in Mathematics but this prize was deservingly awarded to me as I was reputed to be the best mathematical student in the class and Mr. Bhagirath Prasad who was friendly with Professor Sadashiva joked that the best had met the worst as they often do. I was unquestionably the worst Sanskrit student in my class.

After I had got into the senior B.A. Class my brother persuaded me to proceed to Europe for the further prosecution of my studies. The college authorities had also moved that on taking my degree I should be awarded a special scholarship to take my degree at Edinburgh. Professor James Bremner taught me philosophy as I was reading for my degree with honours both in English and Philosophy.

Years later when my college was celebrating its jubilee in 1936 they invited the then living professors to contribute their reminiscences to the Jubilee issue of the Hislopian Magazine. Mr. Brenner had long since retired and was the only professor then alive who could speak of past students from the date of the installation of the College, and he wrote highly of my merits and achievements. In April 1889 I sailed for Europe in charge of my Nephew Murli Manohar Singh. I was then 18 and my Nephew 16. I was readily admitted into my brother's college, Downing College, but Murli was recommended to enter a preparatory school and he joined the Local Leys School.

My brother told me that I must be frugal and that if so Rs. 1100/- P.M. should suffice, but on entering the college I learnt that the least I should have to carry on was £ 200, with the result that I competed for the Mathematical Scholarship of £ 50/- P.A. which I failed to get as the result posted on the Notice-Board read "None Awarded". At the end of my first year I was in deficit to the extent of £ 100 which fortunately I had raised out of the Royalties on my two works, one a book of poems and another a novel to which I shall more fully refer in the next chapter.

CHAPTER III

MY LIFE AT CAMBRIDGE

As stated towards the close of the last Chapter I entered Downing College in the by-term in June but matriculated in the university in October 1889.

I had been living in the college during the preceding vacation, but had to shift to 65 Regent Street on the recommendation of my brother who knew the lessees of those premises by name, Mr. and Mrs. Jackson. Mrs. Jackson was very kind to me for the sake of my brother and I stayed there for a year in the hope that her charges would be met by him as he knew that it was lodging House in the most fashionable street of Cambridge, only a minute or two from the College but when I had to pay to the College and Mrs. Jackson twice the amount I was expecting from my brother I gave up both the college and my lodging and shifted to a cheaper lodging at 58 Hill's Road and Non-Ascription non-collegiate unit of the University. There were over 60 Indians at Cambridge, but the colleges were not then rationed as they have been since. Of all colleges Christ College under the mastership of Dr. Peel wecolmed Indians while Downing, a small College, received them on introduction which my brother gave for messers Alay Mohamad and Mehdi Hasan. The two Nayudus were there before my time while Mr. Tayabji, son of judge of that name, came in afterwards. Trinity, the largest College, had Ranji, the great cricketer and Kumar Ramsinghji, his kinsman. Indians of whatever station in life and in whichever college enrolled complained of their isolation from the white under-graduates. We made a society of our own and had formed a club called the Indian Majlis which is still going strong. Six years ago in 1936 when I was elected to the Chair of the Empire Universities of Quinquennial Conference I was privileged to preside in the very Senate House where 44 years before I had stood as a supplicant for my bachelor's degree. I have been there since and find some little change in the behaviour of the white students whose mentality has undergone noticeable change by the birth of socialism, but the distinction between the white and the coloured students remains, and remain it will till India is free and outlives its inferiority complex. India already knows by now, and knows it too well that the India office with all its employees still carry out the traditional policy of the East India Company. And the worst enemy of India is the India Office. I shall give a few concrete examples of their steady policy towards the young Indians who are thrown to their lap for support and guidance.

I am not indulging in a political diotribe, but for the nonce recording my own view of my own position in England. In my time the students of other countries were under the protecting wing of their national embassies. But India has no such representative, except the Secretary of State for India, and as he is a member (a backbencher)of the British Cabinete, he was necessarily to follow the policy of the British Cabinet which has always been and is to rule India for the benefit of England.

My three years at Cambridge were full of weighty incidents with a year's intensive study in philosophy under the able guidance of Professor Bremner. I naturally aspired to take a degree in Mental and Moral sciences, the tripos of which was said to be proverbially difficult and to which no more than 6 or 8 students sat, and their number remains the same up-to-date. Students in India speak highly of the two great universities of England, but they do not know that they owe their prestige not so much to the difficulty of their curriculum or the intensity of teaching as to the dessimination of social culture, which might be more aptly described as gentlemanliness which the students acquire by consorting with English students of the upper and middle class families who impart their ideals of life and its fellowship to those who may have been brought up in a different atmosphere. Sport affords a fine chance for such close comradeship and it was a common talk that the status of the university for the year depends upon its boat-race, which is a notable London event, next to which is the inter-university Cricket match.

All the students belonging to a College cannot live therein as accomodation for students is limited to about half of those who come in and for the first year or two they have necessarily to live in a boarding house licensed by the University. But all under-graduates are admitted into the college in their third year, which counts, as it is the last year of an undergraduate's stay in the university. In that year most students take their degrees. They invite their mothers and sisters to the May week when the whole University and its colleges are *en fete* and when many departing newly fledged graduates meet their future partners in life.

The university arranges for a set of lectures open to its members on payment of a fee of £ 3-3-0 a term in my time, besides which there are collegiate lectures and above all tutorial classes of 4 or 5 for which the Free was £ 9-9-0 a term.

I spent the first year in preparing for and passing my previous examination. It is nicknamed the "Little Go" against the "Great Go" which entitles one to a degree. In my second year I attended several university lectures in Economics, Moral Philosophy and Logic delivered by Professors Alfred Marshall, Henry Sidgurek and J.M.Keynes. I felt that I had already gone beyond the scope of the lectures and so applied to my tutor to move for my premature admission to the Tripos examination which was permitted and in which I passed with honours, though being only a second year student I was debarred from taking a degree until I had completed my nine residential terms and passed in another tripos. This additional penalty was imposed to keep undergraduates busy in their third year of residence. I took the Law Tripos and taking my degree in June 1892 I decided to return home but how, for I had no money to purchase a ticket. But I had a gold ring about which I have spoken in the previous chapter and a gold watch and chain which I was able to purchase out of the royalty I had earned to which I shall presently refer. All the three were taken to a pawnbrokers who promised to advance £ 17-0-0 thereon which was just enough to purchase third class ticket by a boat taking emigrants to Australia. My nephew Murli who had been with me to the

Dr. Gour at the age of 20

Dr. Gour at the age of 22

pawnbroker offered £ 20-0-0 thereon and took away my golden jewels which he pocketed and left me stranded for my return passage which I had booked and for which the boat-train was to start. The next day I phoned and wired to him but received no response. There was no time to lose and so I saw the manager of the company and persuaded him to detain my baggage till I had paid him my fare in Bombay. But where was I to pay it from I had no idea. I sent a wire to my brother but on arrival in Bombay I found myself without any funds to redeem my baggage. I had with me a gold medal that I had won from the Royal Society of Literature and it was priced at Rs. 40/- a princely sum I thought and so necessary to take me to Hoshangabad where my brother was then practising. I took the first train I could get for Hoshangabad but arriving there next morning I found my brother who received coldly, and it was quite clear to me that I was unwelcome. So I left him by ihe next train for Jabalpur where I knew one or two gentlemen, Messrs Woman Rao Kolhatkar and Harish Chandra Bose, both E. A. Cs and they gladly offered me their hospitality for the few days I had to be there before I should see Mr Antony Macdonell, Chief Commissioner of th Central Provinces. He had the reputation of being an autocrat and all below him trembled to take his name. I wrote to his Secretary Mr. L. H. Laurie for an interview, and much to my surprise and the surprise of the two E.A.Cs Mr. Macdonell consented to see me and which I believe had been achieved on account of the newspaper comments on my books that had preceded me and I was in possession of very commendatory letters from the three renowned professors who had taught me.

As I had made a name as a debator in the union Mr. Macdonell knew something about me and I had sent him with my application for an interview a copy of my book of poems "Random Rhymes" which had drawn a good press. I distinctly remember that the date of my interview was the 21st October, 1892. Mr. Macdonell asked me what I was going to do. I told him plainly that I had come to see him to advise what to do. He said that the utmost he could do for me was to create a vacancy among the E.A.C. and it was the limit of his power. I thanked him and he immediately rang for his Secretary and as I reached my lodgings I received a letter over the signature of this secretary appointing me an officiating E.A.C. and posting me to Bhandara. It created quite a sensation throughout the province and I was flooded with congratulations and offer of help which I thankfully declined. But as I had only one warm suit that I had been wearing I got two cheap cotton suits made costing me Rs. 8/- and started for Bhandara when a fellow Saugorian Radha Nath Dutt brought me his trap and took me home. I stayed with him till I was able to rent a small bungalow into which I moved 3 days after the 20th October, 1892 on which date I took charge of my office as E.A.C. relieving one E.A.C. Mr. Hari Laxman Indurkar who had already left the room as he was suffering from advanced diabetes of which he died. But as he had never applied for leave Mr. Macdonell placed him on compulsory leave for one year and appointed me to officiate for him. My pay worked out to Rs. 229-10-8. Mr. Indurkar had left over a thousand cases undisposed of and I started tackling them with the result that in the Annual, I had disposed of over 880 upto the 26th January 1893 when I tendered my resignation and appeared in a double murder case before Mr. Stanley Ismay who started bullying me by reminding me that I must observe the decorum of the Court by not wasting his time in a lengthy cross-examination to which I replied that I was making a short work of a long case by my cross-examination and so it proved to be. The principal accused in this case was one Madho Banjara who was in charge of a herd of cattle which he grazed as he passed from one market to another. As such he turned them on the village-fields, then full of maturing crop, and the watchman gave alarm whereupon the villagers appeared on the scene, rounded up the cattle and were marching them to an adjoining cattlepound when Madho's men tried to stop them. A free fight ensued in which two of the villagers were killed. The Banjaras took flight and returned to their tanda or camp where they held a council of war and decided upon their line of defence, to support which they set upon an old woman of their own tanda and beat her to death, and then took her body on a charpoy (cot) to the police station house where they found the villagers with two corpses. Each side complained against the other, but the police chalaned Madho and seven of his satellites of murder. They were committed to the Session and were, as already stated, being tried by Mr. Ismay, then feared as strongest Sessions Judge and a terror to the Bar whom he bullied sans ceremonie. The Bar used to treat him as a Superman whose knowledge of law was as deep as it was extensive. But the fact is that he was the only civilian who swore by the English law. Though his knowledge of law was superficial he had certainly made a good use of it. I had taken up this case because the Bar generally had given it up as a forlorn hope and felt so sure of my ground that I took the risk of tendering my resignation of a prize post given to me as a rare compliment by that stern unbending head of the Government which he found steeped in corruption, in efficiency and intrigue and of which the judicial service was packed by promoted clerks, who made hay before their final retirement from the service.

Macdonell was a sworn enemy of these promoted menials and he introduced a distinct service of men whose education and training was some guarantee that they would not follow the shady path of their predecessors.

I was the very first to introduce what was later organized as the Provincial Civil Service and of which Macdonell was the sole progenitor. Mr. Macdonell trusted the educated man and he proved right. To give the C.P. a good turn he imported dozens of members of the I.C.S. and subordinate service but it proved a failure. The provinces he had drawn upon found in it a good opportunity to get rid of their bad bargains, and barring one or two all these exotics failed in the high hopes built upon them. But the local talent proved equal to the high demands made of them, and as my record of Judicial work was put to the test by Mr. Macdonell himself he was gravely dissatisfied when he had to accept my resignation.

But I was anxious to make a name at the Bar of India. I had tried to do so at Cambridge where inspite of my penury and lack of the necessary text-books I had tried to outstrip my fellows

CHAPTER IV

MY CONTEMPORARIES AT CAMBRIDGE

IT seems to be a common failure with all young men to treat their environments as exceptional, and I so regarded mine. From the day of my entry into the university I was struck by the world celebrities by whom I found myself surrounded. Of these I have already mentioned Professors Sidgwick Marshall and Keynes. To that I must add Sir John Seely, Professor Ward and Mr. Besant, a celebrated mathematical coach who had made its possible for one of her girl undergraduates, Margaret Milicent Fawacett, daughter of Mr. Henry Fawcett the economist and the blind Post Master General, ashe was then popularly known, who was placed above the Senior wrangler in the year when I took my degree (1892). Of my contemporaries Mr. Mac Bride became a professor and well-known philosopher. Mr Besant's brother became the husband of Mrs. Annie Besant who with Charles Bradlaugh defied the claries and advocated contraception as more honourable than abortion. She was amongst the pioneers of the Rationalist movement and drew large audiences from the working people. Mr. Bradlaugh was the friend of the down-trodden whether in the field of religion or politics, social economy or labour and he **was the been *ideal*** of the small inconspicuous band of secularists who though free were being still persecuted by the cohorts of medevialists and pseudo-religious fanatics.

From my childhood I had imbibed a longing for freedom in **thought** and action, an unmasked flair for free thought and free expression. And from early life I had nourished a consciousness of my own superiority to my fellow-men, with the result that on my arrival at Cambridge I started speaking at the union, and published a volume of verse in which I had embodied my poem on the Emigrant

Ship which was the subject prescribed for the Chancellor's Golden Medal for English verse for 1890. I competed but failed not because any one else had beaten me but because there was "No Award". My failure at the Mathematical Scholarship and now at the open competition made me suspicious of the University prizes being open to all comers. A hint to the contrary was implied in a casual talk on the subject when my tutor, a reverend gentleman, consoled me by adding that the university was an ecclesiastical institution endowed by ecclesiastical bodies and that we as non-Christian foreigners should be grateful that we were permitted to enter its portals.

The university published two weekly journals "The Cambridge Review" and the "Granta". Of these the one was run by graduates and the other by undergraduates. The university used to have an annual inter-university debate, when all the best speakers on each side had their field-day. I happened to be one of them and reviewing one such debate the Review mentioned me as out and out the best speaker. It is curious that in the year that I am penning these lines (1942) I was invited to speak at Oxford which I did under the Chairmanship of Sir Henry Lawrence K.C.S.I., at one time acting Governor of Bombay, who at the close of my speech declared that he had always thought that Mr. Lloyd George was the finest speaker in the Empire, but he must now revise his opinion and a great deal more to the same effect. But when I stood for the Presidency of the Union I was badly beaten and the only solatium I got was to be unanimously elected to the Presidency of the Majlis. And as for the gold medal I had the solatium of a very eulogizing review from the press.

The financial strain on my scanty leisure drove me to fiction and curiously it was a success. "Letters from Heaven" were written to decry some of the too obvious evils of life and its social structure. It was a bold harrow on man's most intimate relationships which are left to the vagary of chance. I was paid £ 20 as its premium and £ 30 later on and the book sold because of its catchpenny title and not because any one was interested in its earnest appeal for social reform.

I fear all my contemporaries except two or three are now dead.

Of those still alive are F. X. Desouza and Mr. Abdulla Yusuf Ali both ex-members of the Indian Civil Service. Of those no more Ranji became a great Cricketer, Lala Harkishanlal a greater industrialist, C. Krishnan a Judge of the Madras High Court, and last but not the least Aurobindo Ghose a great revolutionary, though while at Cambridge he was scarcely visible being always absorbed in his classics in which he graduated first class. He failed to get into the I.C.S. because he was chucked out of it by a Sergeant Major who refused to admit him to a riding test because he appeared a few minutes later than the time given to him. And the Secretary of State Viscount Cross upheld the Sergeant.

His elder brother Manmohan Ghose was a Gilchrist Scholar at Oxford where he joined in publishing *Primevera* a small volume of verse which was a notable contribution to contemporary Rhyme and to which my "Random Rhymes" purported to be a reply. On his leaving Oxford Manmohan joined Cambridge, where he kept his terms but took no degree. On his return to India he meandered for long till he was appointed a professor of English in the University College, Calcutta. He is now dead. Like a poet Manmohan was an unkempt person with long hair and loose ill-cut coat ; irregular in his habits and uneven in his talk and so was Aurobindo. My Cambridge days were happy but would have been happier if I were not always on the look out for driving the wolf from the door.

The fact that I had taken two Triposes in three years and the fact that my volume of verse had drawn commendation from the British press made my name known in India with the result that on my return to it I was no longer a stranger and the press noticed my return and felt interested in my future. That future was only a larger edition of my past to which I must now turn.

Dr. Gour in his prime

CHAPTER IV

LIGHT IN THE DARKNESS

Upon my return home I had nothing to draw me to my native home. It was to draw me to dear ones. My mother and my younger sister were both dead and so was my father. The house that had been the paradise of my youth stood to remind me of the transitoriness of life. My brother was never the least abstrusive in his affection though in his hate he rent the air with his staccato gunts and "Ha Has". His wife, an uneducated ignorant villager, gave way to her instinctive feelings of motherhood. She was jealous of me for she was afraid that I was getting on while her own son was lagging behind. She made me only too conscious of my inferiority complex in the house. My brother treated her as a household menial which in fact she was and he neglected his own children to whom he talked distantly and whose education he paid for but did nothing more to promote.

As I have said in a previous chapter upon my return to India I had no option but to take up the job of an E.A.C. and after 90 days of service revert to the Bar for which my Temple, the Inner Temple, called me in absentia on the 9th November, 1892. A call in *absentia* is very exceptional and was the subject of press comment. So was my appointment in the two local weeklies, the *Hitavada* published in Harda and the *Deshsewak* in Nagpur. The public of Bhandara took kindly to me as it was the talk of the market-place that the Bar were dumb founded at my disposal, and later on they remarked at the low percentage of reversals of my decision in appeal.

I was able to achieve what I did by closely studying the text books bearing on the subject, in which incidentally I found that the authors, all Englishmen had merely summarised the case-law by setting it out in Chronological sequence. I found this method the very reverse of what a lawyer wants. He does not care to study the subject in its historical perspective but wishes to know what the present law is. A student of law may care to learn how this law came into being, and if he does so he may develop into a deep-read man but not necessarily a ready lawyer. I made notes of all I read and found Mr. Mayne's Hindu Law most faulty. I was surprised that all textbooks on Indian Law bore the impress of English authors, who, as often as not, were not acquainted with the system but only with the case-law which no doubt they had fully mastered. I took a vow that I shall displace every one of them from the market and my legal readers will say to what extent I have not succeeded.

My first venture in this direction was an exhaustive commentary on the Transfer of Property Act, which lays down the law of property in India and on which the standard text-book was the meagre volume produced by messrs Shephard and Brown. My own work on the subject was published n 1895 when I was only 3 years at the Bar, but those 3 years I had utilised in both intensive and critical study of the subject. My work was published by Thacker Spink and Co. and it was sold out in less than six months. The press and the judges acclaimed it as the greatest classic on the subject. The secret of its success lay in the fact that it was not merely a complete repertory of the existing case-law on the subject, which t explained and criticised and the gaps in which it filled up by comments which afterwards went into the cases.

Being only my first essay in the domain of Indian law in which the Indian lawyer paid tribute to the prestige to one of the ruling race I did not price it low but half as much again as any other work on the subject and the volume was twice its size with all doubts solved and conundrums resolved in in a language which was described as crisp and masterly. Several reviews hinted that I must be an old man in my sixties released from the trammels of service, while others opined that the work could not possibly be the product of a single man however acute and eminent. Numerous editions of this work have been called for. The work has now settled down to be, to quote the words of Sir Lawrence Jenkins, "the most authoritative commentary on the Act."

The production of this work prefigured me as an all-India lawyer and I had invitations to shift to Calcutta, Allahabad and Raipur, to which place I shifted because I had known the place during my brother's service there. It was not many days before I became involved in a huge controversy between the Government and the combined Zamindars of Chattisgarh who engaged me along with half a dozen local seniors to protect their status and rights which the Government had noticed them to resume. These cases were put in charge of Mr. Craddock (afterwards Sir Reginal Craddock) who engaged Sir S.P. Sinha, then the Advocate-General of Bengal and the local Government Advocate to oppose the local array of counsel, advocates and vakils who fell out of the team because they felt over-awed by the dazzling array of talent employed against them. I was left alone to fight this cohort and I did so right upto the Privy Council before whom I argued my side of the case for ten days and who complimented the Zamindars' counsel for their able presentation of the case. The case is reported as Raja Brij *Raj Deo V* Secretary of State for India I.L.R. 39 C. 995.

My firmness in standing by my clients when the Government officers had bullied my seniors to throw up their briefs, without refunding the fees that they had taken was much appreciated by my clients who stuck to me and in consequence of which my other brethren at the Bar who had shown their cloven foot at the first sign of necessity became openly jealous of my large practice, which I as a stripling at the Bar had acquired, and which extended to my published work which bamboozled and confused them. All the Government officials declared war upon me as a rebel and a fomenter of litigation which without me would have come to a speedy end, as the Zamindars would then have not even a crutch to lean on though they stood dearly by their rights, their deeds and misdeeds. I fought these cases from start to finish, from the court of origin to that of final appeal, and in the result neither party won or lost as might be judged from the fact that the Privy Council awarded no cost to either side.

Having discharged my responsibility to the Zamindars I left Raipur to conduct a small and ill-paid case in Calcutta where I settled down for a couple of years at 1 Elysium Road, a house I had rented opposite to that of Lord Sinha's at 17 of the same road. But the climate of Calcutta was too damp and hot for me and I got a timely warning from pain in my joints to shift to a drier place which I did, but as Allahabad and Nagpur were both equally dry and Nagpur was the Capital of my Province I naturally migrated to it but not without giving Allahabad a fair chance to hold me if I was so minded. But I found no house large enough to hold my books and I was aghast at the touting system that I had taken root there. Fifty-fifty was the usual rate and my sense of honour and pride resisted any contract with that fraternity. My clerk prophesied that unless I was prepared to fall into line with the rest of my fraternity there was no future for me and his advice came true with the result that I preferred to try Nagpur where that system was still in its infancy mainly because the province was small and poor and the district pleaders advised their clients whom to engage. It did not benefit me as all the litigious districts were in the hand of Bengali Vakils whose parochial patriotism naturally drove them to their two compatriots, Bepin Bose and J. Mitra, after whom I was named. But I very soon discovered that even Bose and Mitra tried to avoid me as an opponent and in cases needing study and argument I was engaged on their side, leaving the other side to Mr. Dillon an Anglo-Indian Barrister who commanded a fair paying practice but who was too lazy to tackle a long case or one involving complexity of accounts with the result that he was equally anxious to get me retained on his side and as it was my life-long rule to take up nothing which I could not thoroughly master I soon found myself surrounded by briefs not only provincial but interprovincial with the result I had to spend months in such places as Lahore, Lucknow and Rangoon, where fresh offers of cases kept me busy most of the time opposed by all the legal talent from Calcutta, Allahabad and Bombay whom I frequently caught napping in spite of the fact that these metropolitan celebrities were often assisted by teams of laborious lawyers whose lucubrations were as confusing as they were pointless.

Lawyers who have penned their own biographies have amused their readers by anecdotes drawn from their professional incidents.

If I were to fellow in their wake I shall need spaces far beyond that occupied by a single volume. But all the same I shall note sohew them. Much of the reputation that I have enjoyed all over India and Burma and latterly in England where I have practised for 5 years in the Privy Council has seemed to come to me *invita Minerva* but on second thought I am convinced that all the serried sparks of the intellect are in essence spontaneous and will not come by study. In this view the rank of Counsel is mostly, if not entirely, due to his inborn genius, though it might be smoothed and polished by study and industry. I could give hundreds of examples to prove my points but in writing this work I imagined that I am giving a fireside to my intimates and I shall, therefore, neither embellish nor dilute the plain facts which I subjoin. My earliest venture into a distance from my natural haunt was brought about in a local case I was arguing before the Judicial Commissioner against the acknowledged leaders of the Bar. The Court room was crowded, and amongst the spectators stood one attentively listening to my voice without understanding a word of what I was saying. He was Rai Sahib Sukhdeo, head Munim of Rai Sahib Seth Chandmal's shop at Damoh known as the Badi Dukan (the great shop) as it happened to be the oldest shop at Damoh and its Munim was the sheet-anchor of his master's numerous shops scattered all over India. One of these at Mian Mir, the Lahore Cantonement, acted as the Government Treasurers in charge of the Lahore Treasury and as such it was the banking firm of many Government officers who had been dealing with it for generations past.

But in 1905 that shop stopped payment and its numerous clients made a raid on the Mian Mir shop to draw their deposits which Chandmal refused to pay on the ground that in a partition between him and his nephews that shop had long been allotted to Dhanrupmal who should be approached for their accounts. The depositors argued that they never had any notice of the partition, and so far as they were concerned they treated the Mian Mir shop as belonging to the family as it was before the so-called partition, which they denied and treated it as bogus to cheat the public. Thirty-five cases were launched against Chandmal and his nephew and a special judge was appointed to dispose them off. All the cases were consolidated by the consent of parties and all counsel joined hands in a single case which was decreed. An appeal by Chandmal was filed by Mr. A. Gray then the leader of the Lahore Bar and President of its Bar Association, who however warned Chandmal that he was leading a forlorn hope. The appeal was set down for hearing before Robertson and Chatterji and Chandmal naturally turned to Calcutta and Bombay for counsel to argue his appeal, but after spending a fortune in paying out the perusal fee he could not secure a single counsel of repute to support his appeal. He had instructed Sukhdeo his trusted confident and Munim of his Damoh shop of his quandary, and Sukhdeo came to me and asked me if I cared to assist Gray who would lead me. I went through his papers and agreed to act and filed three additional grounds to the effect that a public notice given in the press was a sufficient notice to the respondents of the alleged partition. Such notices had appeared in the *Civil and Military Gazette* of Lahore and the *Pioneer* of Allahabad, then the organ of the civil service, copies of which had curiously never been filed.

I went to Lahore a couple of days in advance and had consultation with Mr. Gray and the local counsel. Mr. Gray was despondent and suggested that I should be ready to prove the partition which necessitated my going through a wilderness of 600 account books, all written in the Marwadi character. I spent all the time I had in examining the accounts and found that they showed no separation *in esses* though they purported to show separation *in status*. The Court-room was crowded and with me appeared Mr. Shadilal (afterwards Sir Shadilal, Chief Justice of Lahore and a member of the Judicial Committee of the Privy Council). Being a Bania by caste he naturally knew the Marwadi character and his examination of the books left the issue open. Mr. Gray opened the case and found the judges openly hostile to him. He became boisterous and told Sukhdeo of which Sukhdeo had already found out for himself. He asked me what to do and I told him that Mr. Gray should not close his arguments, but introduce me to carry on which I did. The judges had heard of me as author of the law of Transfer and they were consequently more patient with me than they would have been with a counsel of my standing (I was than a stripling of only 12 years standing). My delivery appeared to have impressed them and after I had given them the summary of arguments in set phrases, they sat up to hear me and after a day's hearing Sukhdeo wired to his maste at Ajmer the following words, "Gray concluded. Court against us. Cour started. Judges coming round". I spent 5 days in my opening after which the court declared that if they decided that the family had become divided in *status* they should not trouble me to wade through the accounts to prove the *quantum* of share alotted to each party and the assets of the several hops brought into the partition.

The respondents who had shoals of counsel began to feel nervous and on the closing day I found the Court clearly in our favour. The appeal was admitted and the legal point I had taken became the subject of a reported case. The appellant had promised me a back fee of Rs. 5,000 out of the costs while he realized to the time of ten times that figure. As the respondents did not carry the case to the Privy Council those cases gave me a great vogue in the Punjab where I was engaged to conduct several *cause celebre*.

As I had proved my things and was returning to Nagpur I was handed a heavy brief from Lucknow which involved interpretation of the local Oudh Estate Act, an Act which has kept more laywers in clover than any other Act on the Statute Book. I had engaged a local lawyer from Nagpur to assist me and he accompanied me to Lucknow, where I was to have been opposed by Sir Sunderlal, doyen of the Allahabad Bar (Stuart C. J. and Ajudhia Nath J. brother of Sunderlal). But on the date of the hearing the Court sent us word that as Sir Sunderlal had taken ill our appeal was adjourned to a fresh date, on which the other side was represented by Pandit Motilal Nehru, as Sir Sunderlal was dead and the sole question at issue was the legality and validity of a will executed by a female Taluqdar under the local Act. The case was argued for 18 days and in the end our appeal succeeded on both the questions of fact and law, and I was offered two more taluquadari cases which, however, I refused as I found them teeming with perjury and forgery. which gave me a closer insight into the affairs of Zamindari which look large and respectable to an outsider but the management of which is in the hands of unscrupulous mercenaries who specialize in poison, corruption, forgery and fraud compared to which the C. P. Zamindaris which though small and scattered are managed by saints. I still remember a case in which the trial Court had found reams of documents all forged for the purpose of proving an adoption—documents not only of the house of the adopter but those of his numerous relations and friends who had inserted items to prove their presents, travelling expenses and the like. And in several such cases which I have handled in appeal I am not sure whether I have been on the right side. For it is my experience shared by other members of my profession that clients and their *qiud nuncs* never give out the truth. They cook up a case between themselves and then proceed to the lawyer to whom they swear their version as the gospel truth and which they engage him to prove.

I have had several such cases in my life, but I would mention one not only because it is typical of the class of such cases but also because it broke down without going to the Court.

In the Chattisgarh there is a zamindari of which Chatter Shah was Zamindar at one time. He had to fight for it but I was successful and for which he naturally felt grateful. His Zamindari had a natural income of about a lac of rupees per annum to which he added another lac by leasing portions of it out to contractors who cut its forest for making sleepers for the Railway. As he had succeeded a lady during whose life-time the Zamindari was managed by the Court of Wards, the estate was in funds to the extent of several lacs of rupees which were made over to Chattar Shah. But Chattar Shah was a simpleton and got himself surrounded by shoals of sharks who started feathering their own nests, and so got into competition with one another. One Chhotelal had managed the estate while it was under the Court of Wards, and he was appointed its manager upon the court relinquishing its supervision and it made all the difference in the world. For while the Government managed the estate Chhotelal was a mere subordinate and had to maintain and submit his accounts to the head manager. And he was watched on all sides so that it left very little scope for his cupidity. But after the official supervision had ceased Chhotelal was all-in-all. He hailed from Narsingpur where he had a battalion of his friends whom he appointed to important posts e.g. Forest Daroga and the like, the result being that the Daroga started falsifying his accounts and passed sleepers upon which no royalty had been paid. Within a few years all the accumulated assets of the Zamindari were exhausted and the forest was being indiscriminately cut to provide the normal royalty and leave the necessary margin for speculation. While the Zamindari was in this state of anarchical confusion Chattar Shah took ill and died, whereupon scenting their dismissal Chhotelal and his myrmidons forged a will purporting to be that of Chattar Shah in which the testator emphasised the necessity of retaining his trustworthy manager in service after his death.

Several copies of this will were made and posted to reponsible officials such as the Commissioner and Deputy Cymmissioner, and one such copy was sent by hand for personal delivery to the Deputy Commissioner. A few hours after Chattar Shah's death the police appeared on the scene and reported that the will was a forgery whereupon the Deputy Commissioner ordered the arrest of Chhotelal, Hospital Sub-Assistant Surgeon and several others who purported to have attested the will. As Chhote Lal was being brought to Raipur he committed suicide. As he was the ring leader his death evaporated all interest in the will, and the estate was once more taken over by the Court of Wards.

I have had to deal with scores of such cases not two of them alike, but cases that drew on me the dawn of life that seemed so impossible to me in my unsophisticated days of innocence and ignorance. And now that I am at the closing chapter of my life I dread to think what a life it has been that I had often to defend, what acts that I had to justify. For example I know of a case in which my moral consciousness openly revolted against my professional duty and I was the means of pulling out of the dock one of the most diabolical criminals it has ever been my misfortune to defend.

This was the case of a Moulvi who maintained a *Muktab* or

school for teaching boys the *Koran*. He had six such boys with two of whom he became unnaturally familiar. These boys of 16 became deadly enemies, but to all appearanaces they were friends. They confessed to each other the crime that the Moulvi was practising on them and they decided to finish the Moulvi for which they borrowed a butcher's knife from a mutual friend. The Moulvi used to invite the boy he fancied for night-study in the Maktab, and on the night in question he invited the boy Mahbub who passed the news on to his friend Isa who was to have appeared when the Moulvi was *flagrante delicto*. But the Moulvi was more astute than his two pupils. He took the boy he had with him for a walk and Isa finding his plan gone astray followed the two and with his knife he first fell upon the Moulvi and having finished him he turned to the boy who had made a run of it as he suspected that Isa was after him for the same purpose. Hosain went to the nearest police outpost and reported all he had seen Isa doing after which he was returning home when Isa set upon him and ejaculating "So you have reported me" chopped off his neck. He too reported his own version of the story which the police recorded after which he was detained.

Next morning the Moulvi's body was sent for a *post mortem*. After due inquiry Isa was chalaned for the double murder of Moulvi and Ishaq. Isha's father was a glass-bangle maker and well-to-do. He engaged me to defend his son, which I did, first on the charge of murdering the Moulvi with his knife which was blood-stained. I pointed out that the Moulvi had certainly been killed by one or other or both the two boys and as there was no evidence to support the last alternative Isa must be acquitted of that charge which he was. But he was convicted of murdering Ishaq upon his own retracted confession which the High Court held insufficient.

This case had got into the press on account of its unsavoury details, and my arguments in the two courts were fully reported. It brought me some *Kudos* and more cases, since it was a case in which the facts certainly pointed to the killing by A or B or A and B; and since there was nothing to prove the killing by the two jointly there could be no conviction of either on proof that one or the other had done the deed.

This was in 1908, when the Zamindari cases were argued before an additional Judicial Commissioner who admitted the Zamindari appeals and modified the District Judge's decree to the extent it was against them. The Secretary of State appealed to the Privy Council and the Zamindars engaged a strong array of Counsel Sir Robert Finlay, Mr. De. Gruyther and myself with Mr. B. Dube. At a conference Sir Charles suggested that after his brief opening I should argue the whole case *in extenso* as I had complete mastery of it and that Mr. De Gruyther should reserve himself for one of the other Zamindars. Sir Charles had recently lost his wife and he was commonly spoken of as the next Tory Lord Chancellor which he became. He was deeply interested in the Declaration of London and frankly confessed to his inability to lead in a lengthy case that might easily go on for a fortnight or more. The arrangement I have mentioned was a compromise that would keep Sir Charles only a day or two out of the House. As it turned out Sir Charles was present only for a few minutes after which he was called away to the House and I had to argue the consolidated cases for a period of ten days. The Judicial Committee was presided over by Lord Macnaughten who bore the reputation of being tempered Irishman, self-opinionated and impatient of argument. I had been previously warned of this by Mr. De Gruyther and I must have done well during the ten days' argument as Lord Macnaughten noted the great ability shown by the appellants' Counsel (*Raja Brij Raj Deo vs Secretary of State, 39 C. 695 P.C.*)

On my return home I found Raipur too small and the cases too dull though I was easily at the top of my profession. I had been in correspondence with Sir Lawrence Jenkins, C.J. of Bengal, who had taken kindly to my books and who welcomed me with open arms as a practitioner in the High Court. I have already given an account of my stay in Calcutta and the necessity that drove me out of it. A vacancy occurred for an additional member of the Viceroy's Council, then opened to a modified form of indirect election by delegates elected by the two local bodies, the District Council, and the Municipalities. Sir Reginald Craddock was then the Chief Commissioner of the Province and he ruled it with an iron hand. He had previously nominated a person who was cent-per-cent pro-bureaucracy and he naturally passed a word round that he was his choice. I was a free lance and treated as a political extremist while a third candidate, the late M.R. Pandit, was put up to divide my vote and it had that effect. Hon. M. B. Dadabhoy secured 23 votes, Gour 15 and Pandit 13.

As I have devoted a special chapter to Politics, I shall hark back to the subject there-at. In 1914 I published the first edition of my Penal Law in two volumes and it was acclaimed as the greatest work on the subject no less for its exhaustiveness than far its literary finish which gave it an international reputation for beyond the area in which the Penal Code itself was in force. Curiously at this time I was engaged in the case of a rich Marwari who was reported to be the common receiver of stolen property. As such the police had long been on the look out for him till they seized a valuable junk of gold and silver which he said he had taken in pawn from persons who could not have stolen them and for which they were convicted and two of them transported as they were shown to have been guilty of a political dacoity.

The accused was a well-known nationalist and highly idolised by young India. He was spectacularly demonstrative of his political largesses. A strong array of Counsel were engaged to bring him to book, and the district magistrate took up the case himself for trial.

He examined scores of witnesses to prove the owners of the several ornaments, and the prosecution began to indulge in cheap jokes at such a small mouse coming out of such a mountain. When it came to my turn to argue I was in a quandary, as I was not sure the Magistrate would not make good the serious gap the prosecution had left in the case without which the accused could not be convicted. And the Magistrate had the power to fill in such lacunae under section 540 of the Criminal Procedure Code. So I put the Magistrate upon his honour, reminding him that the prosecution were well represented by expert Criminal lawyers, and if they had failed to bring the charges home to the accused the Court should not run to their rescue. The Court promised that it would do nothing of the kind. I then took the risk and informed the Court that my client was entitled to be acquitted as there was no evidence in the case that the jewels in question were stolen property, whereupon the leading prosecutor jumped up to his feet and hurled at my face a copy of the judgment of the High Court upholding the conviction of dacoity, and he added that some of the jewels now in Court were exhibits in that case and showed to have been the subject of the dacoity.

I pointed out that the said judgment and the said trial were wholly irrelevant in that no finding not *inter partes* bound my client who remained free to challenge a finding to which he was no party. It was a poser to the prosecution who became excited and clamorous, and in the end filed a petition for the examination of additional witnesses to prove the point I had taken as fatal to the prosecution. I drew attention of the Court that I had closed my defence and the prosecution their case. There was a power in the Court which should not be used to implement the prosecution. The Court declined to reopen the prosecution and the accused was acquitted. It created a great sensation and the prosecution moved the local Government to appeal against the acquittal but the local Government did not appeal.

I had by now (1919) became an All India practitioner and was as much in demand in civil as in criminal cases, and I had by now fixed my daily fee at Rs. 1,000 with Rs. 3,000 as the minimum. As such I have appeared in several cases in the High Court of Calcutta, Patna, Allahabad and Lahore and in the Chief Court of Lucknow, not to mention the High Court of Hyderabad, Indore, and several Indian States. But a casual chance took me to Rangoon where I was said to have made a great name by securing the acquittal of Mr. Joseph, at one time a millionaire timber contractor who had undertaken to supply ten lacs of sleepers to the B.N. Railway who were the pooling agents of several Indian Railways. Mr. Joseph had taken lease of the Burmese forest from Government, and his mode of supply to the Railway was as follows. A European passing officer used to visit the timber depot and pass such sleepers as he approved by impressing on them a hammer mark, which he took away with him as soon as the passing was over. After several such examinations Mr. Joseph found that the Railway Engineer was too critical of his sleepers and had rejected as many as 40 per cent of those spread out for his passing. Mr. Joseph was a Madrasi Christian and had employed a Mr. Mudaliar as his agent to represent him.

This Mudliar used to keep a book in which the number of passes were noted by him. It showed so many rejections that Mr. Joseph took fright that his contract would result in a heavy loss to him. So according to the prosecution supported by the accomplice testimony of Mudaliar Mr. Joseph had a copy made of the passing hammer and forged a false one with which he started passing the rejected ones on which he was paid as much as on those legitimately passed. It seems that some one warned the B. N. Rly. Company of the swindle they were paying for, which on examination they found to be correct. They reported the matter and Joseph was prosecuted and sent to jail for a period of 4 years. Mrs. Joseph, a clever Kashmiri Pandit's daughter, had read my name in the papers. She had sent her local Barrister the usual plea for such help, but no one of repute in Calcutta would consent to handle her case, whereupon she fixed on me and I agreed. The appeal was heard by Bagley J. and the Railway Company had engaged all the local talent and in addition sent a leading counsel from Calcutta. On the first day the Court was so over-crowded that Mr. Bagley had to request the Chief Justice for his own room in which the appeal was heard. The hearing lasted 12 days, after which the court reserved judgment. Mr. Joseph had already been released on bail and he was warned to appear on a date to be notified. It was clear from the failure of the prosecution to meet my point that there was only one verdict possible in appeal and it could be no other than one for acquittal which was given a fortnight later on the ground that Mudaliar was an accomplice and his evidence required to be but was uncorroborated and that he had a motive of his own to forge the hammer because Joseph had threatened him with dismissal on the ground that there were too many rejections of sleepers. A very important case relating to the oil-wells between an Indian and the Rangoon Oil Co. was then being tried by the High Court and I was engaged by the Indian firm to defend his right. The case involved complicated details of no general interest to the public, but boldly speaking the Rangoon Co. complained that Sir Kasam, the Indian Oil King of Burma, had opened a well on a lower level to the Company's well with the result that their own well was drying up. My point was the distance between the two properties on which we were successful.

My visit to Burma introduced me to many clients who have since requisitioned my services in many cases, added to which I visited it for a month or so as a member of Simon Commission. The fact that I had fixed my headquarters at Nagpur had some effect in discounting my value both as a lawyer and an advocate, because the litigating public could not realize why a lawyer of my reputed rank and position had for his headquarters a small provincial town with not even a High Court and my friends outside the legal circle must be equally perplexed, because legal practice in Nagpur, and for that matter in the Central Provinces and Berar, is not worth Rs. 3,000/- P. M., my usual daily fee in Burma. But the truth is on my return from Calcutta to Nagpur I could not find a sufficiently large house for my books and I had therefore no option but to build one which I did in a four acre of garden land where I was able to accomodate my large Library and as at the same time I had had it designed according to my taste and wants. Having settled down comfortably in this home I felt no desire to abandon it. I had rented 1 Elysium Row in Calcutta and another house in Allahabad, but I was never half so comfortable in either, and unless I could see another house in Calcutta or Bombay I should not be able to overcome my first objection, but then the question of climate would remain. It had driven me out of Calcutta, and it might do the same from Bombay; while there was not much to choose between Allahabad, Lahore and Nagpur—at least so, I thought when I was instinctively disinclined to shift. So inspite of my handicap and lowered prestige I continued to date my letters from Nagpur, till I left it in April 1938 England for where I had been to take silk of which details will be found given elsewhere. Finding myself thrown into a life of forced idleness on account of the war and the growing risk of a sea-passage home and the dearth of an air-passage to one proceeding on no public duty, I thought that I might well employ such leisure in jotting down the main events of my life which I have accordingly done. To resume the chain of events.

In my previous resume I have brought my life upto the first Great War on the close of which Mr. Montagu as Secretary of State for India paid a visit to India to study on the spot the question of what post-War reforms India should receive. He paid a visit to the principal provincial capitals, and fixed the 1st of January, 1918 for an interview with me and my colleague Mr. Vishnu Dutt Shukul of Sihora. In our written memorandum, noted by Mr. Montagu in his Diary, since published by his widow "as one of the ablest presented to me in India" we gave a sketchy account of the Anglo-American negotiations since published by Mr. Lloyd George, which resulted in the British Government's declaration that they had abandoned Imperialism and would no longer govern a country without the consent of the governed, and as India had long been clamouring for self-rule, Mr. Lloyd George invited India along with the seven white colonies to a special conference to receive self-Government, both internal and external which was formally embodied in the 9th Resolution of the Imperial War Conference dated 16-4-17.

I asked Mr. Montagu whether that pledge would be made good and he said that he was there to do so. Lord Chelmsford was then the Governor-General of India and our interview lasted about 35 minutes. But contrary to our expectations the pledge of 16-4-17 was not only jettisoned, but the British Government substituted therefore the pledge of the 17th August 1917 which completely negatived the broad declaration of 16-4-1917.

I wrote a series of articles in the press but the Government propagandizers proved too strong for me. They described me as an impatient extremist who was driving India ahead of such old democracies as Canada and Australia. And though the Congress did not make my point their own, they complained of the mockery of the Act of 1919 which they decided to boycott and with it the Councils that it had created.

I was by no means enamoured of the Councils, but advised the Congress not to boycott them as it would give the sycophantic group a chance to go in and so blunt the Congress demand. The question came up before the Nagpur Session of the Congress, and as I had been by then returned unopposed to the Indian Legislative Assembly, members of the C.P. Provincial Committee of which I was the chairman began to feel that I was defying the Congress and I felt that I was. This was in December 1920 and I accordingly withdrew from the Congress in the Working Committee of which I was grossly outvoted. The temper of the Subjects Committee was even more truculent and after Mahatma Gandhi's speech men like Pandit Madan Mohan Malviya were shouted down and so was I. The adoption of the boycott resolution by the Congress was a mere formality and the country became sharply divided into pro-council and anti-Council parties. Unfortunately for me, four of my other colleagues were duds and as the other provinces had followed suit I found to my surprise that the first Indian Legislative Assembly comprised members who had no claim to understand politics, but who had taken advantage of the boycott of coming to make hay or atleast to gain Kudos by their distinction as members of the Central Legislature.

In the Chapter relating to my political service I have set out at length such history as I could make of the Central Legislature from 1921-1935. I may add here that in spite of its obvious infirmity and drawbacks as representing only moderate India, the first Assembly has the credit of enacting such important measures of social reform as the Inter-Caste Marriage Act (Act XXX of 1924) and Women's Freeom Act and several other Acts to which reference will be found made in sequal.

Here I wish to add that the bureaucratic Centre took full advantage of the weak and docile legislature to carry out their own policy in the name of the people whose nominal representatives in the Central Legislature were only too willing to sell their souls for a mess of pottage.

I tried to form an organized opposition and succeeded in obtaining its official recognition, but lacking the two essential weapons of power—reward and punishment, I was a mere leader of my party and the opposition, but the Government knew the hollowness of my position and the shallowness of my party—the Democratic Party which had the nominal headroll of 43 members, but of which I could not be certain of a single one, with the result that I could not take a firm stand on any question of policy on which we and the Government were sharply divided. But following the mode of the British Parliament we kept up the semblance of a so-called opposition which became real and efficient in the later twenties and thirties when the Congress took our place, though they went to the other extreme of boycotting the meetings though not the form.

As one deeply interested in the reform of Hindu Society I was deeply interested in the reform of Hindu law which affected and controlled it through all stages of a Hindu's life. I thought that no Hindu will listen to the reformers voice to reform a law when he does not know what it is. Hindu law was nowhere to be found; neither in the library of a hundred scriptures written in Sanskrit which has always been a dead language alive only for use of the *Pundits*, since the texts of these ancient books have been interpreted out of their obvious meanings by scores of commentaries and in later days by as many decided cases; the result being that Hindu law was like a rare metal buried deep in the bowels of the earth only to be unearthed by the lucky pleader with some knowledge of Geology.

I wished to bring this law to the door of the common man, and for that purpose codified it in sections, a feat acknowledgedly considered impossible for 300 years. The next thing I did was to draft a few reforming Bills correcting some of its most patent vagaries which I distributed to all members of my party since a chance to push on a Bill is by the rules of the Legislature left to ballot and one who wishes his Bill to come on to a certainty has to get it countersigned by as many members as he can get. It does not matter if they know nothing about it and if they draw they need not move since they can authorise another member to do so. In the 14 years that I was a member of the Legislative Assembly I was able to place on the Statute Book a large number of Bills, both official and my own the latter exceeding those that all the other members were able to enact during the same period.

Apart from the Bills I was a member of the Statue Law Revision Committee, which after a period of some activity came to a sudden end, as the bureaucracy dreaded its growing power and encroachment on its own authority. I say this because I had suggested the elimination of judicial conflict upon several points of interpretation of the Statute and personal laws, which wasted the time of the Courts and money of the litigating public without making them any the wiser, and as will be seen in the Chapter specially devoted to Legislation, I was still able to correct some of the glaring errors of the Lords of the Privy Council who being the ultimate court of appeal are regarded by the Bar as both conceited and slip-shod, and I regret to have indorsed this view with my 5 years' practice before them.

In my 50 years of public life I have occupied many stages and played many parts, but have never for once and ever so short a time served as an "official", so that my life, though versatile, cannot be described as to that extent varied. But such as it is I have tried to set out in topical details in the ensuing chapters.

CHAPTER V

MY LIFE AS AN AUTHOR

FROM the earliest period of my life that I can remember, and my memory takes me back to the age of five, I was fond of constructive originality and invention. In our house on Sanicheri Touri there was scarcity of water as it had to be handled up from the wells in the valley or the great lake about half a mile downhill, say a 100 feet below the apex of the hill where our house was situated. A waterwoman sold water both drinking and washing at one anna a chetty per month. But as we needed atleast 20 such chetties every day it meant Rs. 1/4/- P. M. to which my parents could afford, when I was 5-10 and their allowance at the highest figure of Rs. 50/- P. M. But as my brother's family multiplied, and so did ours, our allowance was consequently reduced to Rs. 30, Rs. 20/- and Rs. 10/- P. M. My mother became naturally growingly economical, with the result that she and I had frequent quarrels over my waste of her water in a tiny garden that I had planted from the age of 5 and which when I was 10 had grown into a field about 20 ft. square with small ornamental road and boulevards six inches and a foot wide in which grew radishes, gram, maize, cobs and cucumbers in the cold season and the monsoon while in the days of mid-April to mid-June I grew Jasmine and other flowers for which my mother grudged the water of which the thirsty earth used to swallow chetties-ful and on the top of it all I had an ornamental central reservoir which being a thirsty ditch about 6 inches in diameter and about a foot deep needed constant replenishment of water for which I had to run to our family water-stand for a supply. This waste of water was wanton, but my mother never once resorted to physical force to stop it. The fact seems to be that her own blood was agrarian and she took my boyish prank as by no means unnatural in the offspring of a

Dr. Gour as practising lawyer at Rajpur

Dr. Sir Hari Singh Gour (1929)

generation of clodhoppers. This craving for maintaining a garden or a field and growing on it a variety of crops of which I could procure the seeds remained unacted by the fall in our revenue and the increase in my parental obligations, for not only had my father since my birth another daughter, but his second son was growing up and had to be sent to school while my own admission into the Kindergarten *Pathshala* was a gentle reminder of the necessity of thrift. But my father too never interfered with my agricultural ventures ; on the contrary he relished them, though he formally granted his assent to my mother's complaint about water As I grew in years I tried my hand at weaving out of skin strips watch-chains, bags and I turned an old tin-pot into a water clock by boring a hole in its bottom which drowned the tin in a bucket in what I think was 25 minutes according to Ganpat's pocket-watch which was an English Lever, the paragon of perfection of watches in the 'eighties. I remember my brother Ganpat making fun of my tinpot clock and adding that it sank only in 25 minutes. He suggested how to reduce the hole which I did but it then began to sink in 31 minutes. I was never able to regulate it any more. I did other boyish freaks but they were all the outcome of my passion for invention. While at Cambridge I invented a fountain pen but my invention, though on the right lines, lacked finis of technique, which by the way is still lacking since all the known models are either dependent on vacuum or suction which does not insure free flow of ink and freedom from blotting. I have made such a pen and have done much writing with it, but I find it to clog at times and this I am now trying to eliminate. But two devices that have been patented and won universal acclamation are a shaving razor and a self-propelling knife, both of which have been patented both in England and in India, and both of which would have been manufactured on a commercial scale but for the War.

Turning from mechanical to intellectual invention I composed some verses, I blush to recall, when I was 10 and in 1887 I composed mnemonic verses to memorise some logical formula. Two years later I composed and competed for the Chancellor's gold Medal for English verse, the subject for that year being "An Emigrant Ship".

The poem "Stepping Westward" was included in my volume of verse "Random Rhymes" of which I had a good press and appreciation from well-known public men, which however, I dismissed as merely courteous phrases. I have already mentioned that I did not win the medal as there was "No Award". I did not make any money on the publication of this maiden volume, but it encouraged me to compose a volume of prose, styled "Letters from Heaven" in which I depicted the absurdity of some of our customs, habits and conventions that still survive and are treated as badges of good breeding though they violently warp us from the living truth. I received the premium of £ 20 from the publishers but no royalty. The letters were published in the Provincial Press. The growing exactions of the several examinations I was preparing for placed a curb upon my literary activity until my return to India, when with the very first year of my practice I vowed to outdo Maine, Shephard and Brown, and in 1912 published the first edition of my Law of Transfer which was acclaimed as a classic by the highest legal authorities of the time such as Sir Lawrence Jenkins, and apart from their opinions, though no doubt partially because of them, the whole edition of one thousand copies was exhausted within three months of its publication, a record for a legal work in the nineties when seven years was the average life of a legal publication. But apart from it my work has so stopped the sale of Shephard and Brown's commentaries that the publishers had to reduce their price from Rs. 15/- to Rs. 5/-; while my work was issued at Rs. 20/-. The second edition published in three volumes had a similar sale and so have the later editions.

Encouraged by the phenomenal success of this first legal venture I attempted to outdo all commentators on the criminal law of India by publishing my commentary in two volumeəs thereon, styled "The Penal Law of India." This work, extending as it does to about 3000 pages, is by far and away the largest work on criminal law in the English language and its sale has been world-wide. It is now in the fifth edition, and the Law Quarterly Review has spoken of it in high terms. Till 1910 the greatest work on Hindu Law was that by Maine who sold his small demy 8VO volume of about 500 pages at Rs. 20/- a copy. Maine had collected all the matter put into his work as a member of the committee appointed by Government to codify the whole parts of Hindu Law which Mr. Maine described as a miracle and the age for miracle is passed. When I read this in his preface, as also the fact that Mr. James Mill in his History of India pressed on Parliament the necessity of clarification of the labyrinthine confusion of what was euphemistically described as "Hindu Law" which every one legally presumed to know and which the Courts were presumed to unerringly administer and yet there was scarcely a point upon which conflicting texts could not be found and conflicting decisions not given.

Aurangzeb had appointed two committees of the Pandits and the Moulvis to codify the personal laws of the Hindus and the Moslems. The Moslems did it in the Fatwa-i-Alamgiri, but the Hindus could not. The E.I.Co. appointed two committees to do it but one of them made the confusion worse confounded by merely selecting some texts which they set out under appropriate heads, but while this committee eliminated conflicting texts, it failed to see that the texts they had selected were themselves ill-drawn by the Pandits who having lacked the precision and accuracy of a lawyer had loosely worded them with the result that they in their turn became the targets of legal logomachy and judicial aberrations. Sir William Jones and Macaulay each tried his hand at its codification and each failed till another commission was appointed under the chairmanship of Sir Arthur Hobhouse of which Maine was an accredited member. After 5 or 6 years of devoted labour they threw up the task as a forlorn hope, till I essayed it single-handed and published what is acclaimed as a perfect code. It is not perfect in the sense of being good law, but it is perfect in the sense that it is couched in a language which is both clear and unambiguous, digestive and exhaustive. The following are some of the lines occuring in a lengthy review of the fourth edition of this Code: "To those who know the genial author every page of this book will bring reminiscences of the gusto with which his active mind leaps forward from one dialectial proposition to another and to the one after that. Those who do not know him may be tempted to wonder how a work so full of superficial blemishes can ever achieve the position of authority which it unquestionably has: Althoug the author is happily still with us[1], the work is habitually quoted in the Privy Council and in all the High Courts, a triumph to merit not easily earned and no library of Hindu Law would be complete without it. The fact is that Sir Hari Singh Gour is very much like once of the great rivers of India in the monsoon. The holy waters sweep by in one great flood, and the troubled surface hides the depth and strength of the current. We would not willingly baptize a beginner in Gour ; but those who know enough about the subject to keep their heads above water can hardly read even a few pages of this book without being stimulated and without feeling that they have received new ideas and a point of view which is definitely the author's own"[2] Following the wake of this work the Government have appointed another committee to codify the whole or parts of Hindu Law and that Committee is at the present moment engaged upon that work. In addition to the legal works I have published several volumes of *Belles letters* including an exhaustive work on "The Spirit of Buddhism" (1929) which Mahatma Gandhi has eulogised as the greatest work on the subject and for which Rabindranath Tagore penned a foreword. It is most sumptuously illustrated and gorgeously decorated work and gives to the wide public outside India some idea of the capacity of the Indian press. Messrs Luzac and Co. are the publishers of its overseas edition which has commanded a fairly wide sale. A novel dealing with the subject of women in India and called "His only Love" was issued about the same time, but as its publisher turned bankrupt soon after its publication the work never had a fair deal. It discouraged me to publish other books, chapters of which I have moulded into magazine articles in which form they have been published. But descending as they have done to the low level of fugitive literature, they have not had the large circle of readers that a published work can command.

Some of my articles in the magazines have been of what is

---

1. Refers to the practice that the work of a living author should never be quoted as authority.

2. 55 Law Quarterly Review, P. 610.

commonly described as Rationalist in thought and expression, and as such they have been eschewed by the monthlies of standing though their editors have not failed to add their appreciation of them but have excused themselves on the war-scarcity of paper. They have, however, appeared in the *Calcutta Review* through which, I trust, they may have reached the young formative mind of India.

Turning from the written to the spoken word I was from early life gratified to find my speeches applauded and admired by the audiences to whom they were addressed. I have from the stage of my adolescence visited and delivered speeches in almost all parts of the world—old and new. In the 'eighties I was a frequent speaker in the union, and spoke on the occasion of the inter-university debate held once a year when the *Cambridge Review* noted that as a speaker I was all-in-all the best of them all. In later years (in 1942) I had occasion to deliver an impromtu speech at Oxford when Sir Henry Lawrence K.C.S.I. I.C.S. (Retired), acting Governor of Bombay, presided. In his closing words he said that he had up to the moment I had got up to speak thought that Mr. Lloyd George was our best speaker in the Empire, but after hearing me he was of the opinion that I was as much superior to Lloyd George as Llyed George was to the rest of them. I do not pen these fino phrases to make my readers take them literally, but I have done so to impart to my friends the momentary glamour that my speeches have at times created in my hearers. I have by now delivered on thousands of occasion, to all kinds of audiences, big and small, young and old, educated and rustic, lay and learned, but I have never for a moment felt any difficulty in giving expression to my views, palatable or otherwise, in a language, crisp, clear and ornate that has without the least effort come on my tongue and I am thankful I have often asked myself a question whether my straight-forward writings and talk have had any effect upon the public. I answer none so far as I can felt.

And the only reason that I can give is that the public are too obedient to authority and power that my speeches and writings being of a free-lance, never in power, have failed to create any impression upon the people at large or any section or unit of them so far as I can judge. And what is more, they have failed to create any impression upon my own children, who are temperamentally as far from me as the poles asunder.

Judging as impartially as I can, they have, one and all, more taken after their mother than myself. My wife was fond of frivolity and drink and so are all of them. I eject this thought with great reluctance, but I have done so for the sake of Truth.

Barrister Gour

Dr. H. S. Gour : as The Vice-Chancellor

CHAPTER VI

MY LIFE AS A POLITICIAN

As I was fond of debate and discussion in my school days I naturally looked forward to an opportunity when I should be able to display my talent to a greater advantage. That opportunity presented itself when I was in Bhandara in 1893 in the summer of which there was a general election to the Municipality. I was then living in a ward known as the "Tikka Para" which was a corner of the city nearest to the civil station in which were situate all the offices and in which all the European and some Indian officials lived. Bhandara was then, as it is now, a district and the principal administrator of it was the Deputy Commissioner, who ran the whole district as its little monarch, in whom all powers, civil, revenue and general centred. He was nominally under a Divisional Commissioner, who however was a confirmed believer of trusting a man on the spot. One of my first escapade with the then Deputy Commissioner was forced upon me by my own conscience which had been from early life enjoining me to follow the Truth and defy the consequences. This is now expressed by the compound word *Satyagrah* which is the moral passward for all Congressmen, but who observe it in a way of their own. The Deputy Commissioner, Lawrie by name, followed the hackneyed tactics of his order. He had a large room set apart for him in the main office-building, but following the rule of the civil service he scorned to use it, but did his official work in his own bungalow, where he equally tried such cases as he cared to take up. Having joined the Bar of about 20 members I found myself relegated to the Bar-room which was an enclosed corner of the verandah of the Kacheri about 15×10 in which there was spread a torn and ragged carpet with two or three cushions covered with duck which had gone through many coloured phases till the superimposed coating of dust had wholly obscured them. It was the rule in the Bar that it should be used only by members of the learned profession who were legitimately entitled to use it, and which meant members who were not in arrears with their monthly subscription of Re. 1/- out of which a peon retained on Rs. 8/- P.M. was paid but as almost every member was in arrears with his dues that rule had become a dead letter, and as it left the Library in debt to the peon, the latter made good his wherewithal by acting as a tout to several members, and as he was so busy he used to come to the Library—so called, though it had no books except a *panchang* or *a vernacular* calendar of which those for several years were kept tied up to assist members in computing limitation and informing them of the holidays. All the members of the Bar except myself were Marathi Brahmins and all of them came in *Chappal* or half-slippers which they left in the verandah. When I joined the Bar I found it out of sort with my habit of donning European clothes and boots I could not squat on the floor with the rest of them and with their permission I brought in my own chair and a big table that I squeezed into a corner. But I found it soon turning into a common table and as I was shocked with the spectacle of the Bar Library I decided to present it with soft cushioned settees and a table fitted with ink and pens and writing, sundries, such as blotting pad, a weighing machine, a gum pot and the like. As the only Barrister. I stood above the vakils who elected me as their president and in return I cleared the peon's arrears of pay and employed a *punkha* coolie to cool the members in the hot days. The litigants who had no waiting room used to squeeze into the Bar rat hole, but I put up a notice "Members only" and ordered the peon to remain at his duty and keep intruders out.

Only within a month or so after my joining the Bar there was a general election to the Municipality, the office-bearers and members of which were the *de facto* nominees of the Deputy Commissioner who ran both the local bodies, the District Council and the Municipality, the local boards and its adjutant bodies, the school-board, the sanitation Committees and the like. I decided that this long-suffering mockery of local self-government should cease and that the people should be taught to use their own judgment in the elections, instead of supporting the "Sarkari candidate" which had become the unwritten law of the land. I held a meeting of the Bar to lend me support which it di as nonchalantly as they would have done the contrary. The fact is that their civil self-consciousness was then dormant. It had not been roused by reflexion. They were all greybeards with no vestige of personality, and many among them were anxious to be the first to inform the Deputy Commissioner of my seditious preaching. But as it was, secretly though not so openly as before, the Deputy Commissioner passed his fiat, and as such fixed upon one Anwar Ali as the Sarkari candidate from the Civil Station cum Tikka Pura in which I had rented a house and in which I had enrolled myself as a voter. Bhandara had then a population of 35,000 but I doubt if I could get one man among them to say that the people should not deny themselves their right of self-government. This idea was both novel and strange to all of them, and when I went about holding meetings and telling the people of what self-government meant and cow it would develop, they gave me their courteous approval, but did not know what I was taking about, much less what I wanted them to do. If I had asked one of them to paraphrase my speech he would have done it by saying that I was asking them to defy the *bada Sahib*, that is all. But it was not all. On the contrary their defiance would not have come in if the Bada Sahib had not defied the Local Self Government Act which wanted all elections to be free elections. But there it was. It is not what I said but what the people understood that counts and the D.C. and myself were already at daggers drawn when another incident brought me in direct conflict with him. As I have said before the D.C. did all his work, judicial and non-judicial at home. As such he had a case in which a pleader Mr. Jageshwar Rao was defending. He went to the D.C.'s room with his slippers on whereupon the D.C. burst forth into one of his paraxysms calling the pleader a Damned *Soor* and ordering him out of the room. Poor Jageshwar obeyed, but on returning to the Bar Library he reported to the members the occurrence whereupon the members appealed to me for redress. Without a moment's hesitation I went to the common table and dashed off a peremptory complaint and demanded a written apology. The D.C.'s feelings on this letter can better be imagined than described. But as I received no acknowledgement of my complaint or any apology I dashed of a complaint to the Divisional Commissioner Mr. John Neill who approached Mr. John (afterwards Sir John) Woodburn who had succeeded Mr. Macdonald as officiating Chief Commissioner.

What passed behind the scenes I do not know, but the D.C. was later transferred to Wardha and his place taken by a young Assistant to whom the departing D.C. must have coached up about this and other events in the district. But the Municipal elections came on before the D.C. left the district and the polling officer of the Tikka Para was a Naib Nazir and the time for elections from 8 to 11 A.M. just two minutes after which there arrived the D.C. with all his menials to vote for Anwar Ali. I protested and the polling officer showed his watch to the D.C. whereupon the D.C. and his seven satellites quietly turned their backs—not that if they had voted I would not have been returned for I had scored 43 votes against Anwar Ali's 20.

As he was on transfer the D.C. appears to have lost all interest in Bhandara, for out of 14 members newly elected there were only 6 *Sarkāri logs*, the remainder were men of no decided bias. In the nineties a man was looked upto as one possessing some influence if not power if he was in the good books of Government and contrari wise a man against the Government was looked down upon and avoided by the public. I had already been denounced as *par excellence* of the latter class, though curiously my practice did not suffer on that account. It began at the top and remained there for about 2 years that I stayed in Bhandara. I have since been informed that no one has reached the mark of Rs. 2000 P. M. after me, but in fairness to my Bhandara friends I must mention that that figure was inclusive of large touting practice in the neighbouring districts not excluding those of Chhattisgarh. As this practice became more pressing I had ceased to take any interest in the municipal and district council elections of which I remained a member and R.B. Yadao Rao Paikan Pande, a money-lender from Kanpur who was the Government nominee was again re-elected to the chair of both, and I have reason to believe that even if I had tried to oust him I would not have succeeded as his monetary and official influence—both combined could not be attacked by any one not so well circumstanced. On the 26th January 1893 I had started my practice with a double murder case before that bully Stanley Ismay. By June 1894 I had shifted to Raipur where the agents of the Zamindar of Fingeshwar, Babu Mohanlal and Gaibi Nath Chaube, pressed me to rent a house and they promised me ample work for which I had at no time to wait. But though I had shifted to a better place and had taken up some important cases the value of my practice never went beyond the Bhandara figure till after 1911 when I returned home after finishing the Privy Council cases. But the reasons for my *ad interim* stagnation was not the want of cases but the severity of competition and unprofessional intrigues to drive me out of Raipur. As will be easily recalled the cream of practice in those days was in all districts in the hands of Bengalis who had a well-developed sense of communal patriotism and who being intellectually superior to the local talent had not difficulty in holding their own. When, therefore, I came to Raipur the four or five Bengalis who had all the practice of Sadar Bazar and the Zamindars were alarmed at my having captured one of their Zamindars, and through his virile agents I had captured many more ; with the result that I was faced with several petitions under the Legal Practitioners Act complaining of my misconduct in having received a house (valued at Rs. 300) from Shri Durga Das Bairagi as my fee promising to return it to him if I lost the case, which I did. But I had made no promise, and though Mr. J. N. Sircar, doyen of the local Bar, had lodged the complaint and Babu Ambica Charan Ghosh swore to it, their cross-examination by me brought out the fact of a conspiracy to hound me out of their Jagir. Mr. M. W. Foxstrangways the D.C. refused to go on with the case which was curiously dismissed in default, but this did not close the crop of cases which began to be filed before [the District Judge ; but fortunately for me the people no less than the Judges understood the nature that lay behind these cases which were made a short shift of in the course of two years by when I had acquired sufficient professional reputation and influence to fear such attacks.

but these failing a foul cause was started that I was dishonest and took up briefs from both sides. The only truth in these attacks was that I had started the practice of charging Rs. 5 for consultation and it often happened that I had to advise a person not to file an appeal and if he did so as he often did I appeared for the respondent whereupon an application was filed that the appellant had confided to me his case and its secrets and that therefore I was professionally guilty in appearing against him. Any way the rumour was kept alive for some time, and were it not for the fidelity of a few of my clients to combat the rumour it would have assuredly put me out of bounds. In the decennary 1894-1904 in which these scenes were enacted I happened to publish my first legal work which took the legal world by storm. It also counteracted the rumour which in course of time died a natural death. But I am sorry to have to add now as a bare historical fact, my success at the bar and as an author did in no way mitigate the professional jealousy and its darts to which I was subjected. In all these years I had not a single friend in the ranks of my profession, since the bulk of them were afraid of the leaders whom they dared not oppose even in thought or expression.

I overcame the marshalled forces of opposition by my work and example with the result that the clients who came to me by chance stayed with me by design and they combated the libellous imputations against my professional and personal character that the touts of my opponents had been inventing and passing current, the more so because I had steered clear of all touts, noble and ignoble, and relied upon my patience and hard work for success.

What this means let me say for the benefit of such of the youngsters as may like to emulate my example. From early life I was a hard student and eschewed all idle pastimes including games. I calculate that when I was studying for my matriculation and my degree I did not compute my work by the hours I had devoted to it, but by the concentrated attention I had paid to it. As for the hours I have on an average worked about 8 hours a-day and I consider it ample for any examination or study. At the Bar I followed the same rule only adding an hour or two if I found that I had not been able to give undivided and concentrated attention within the usual period. I have always given an hour for walking in the fresh air. I have been a life-long abstainer from wine and women and all petty pleasures of life, shows and cinemas, dancing and music, employing my spare time in reading books of additional value. My curiosity has rivetted my attention to the weighty problems of life and death, the universe, its constitution and composition, its ultimate cause and creator and its immediate and ultimate objective.

On these and kindered subjects I have read largely books by authoritative writers and written books and articles of my own, but which do not seem to attract the common people, who are content to believe in the consoling dogmas of faith and follow its precepts with unswerving loyalty. As these people are not able to go beyond the narrow track of their mental outlook it is idle to drag them into the hard facts of science. I have thus been cut off from all congenial social contact and my whole life has passed in my own company undiversified by social conventions of a work-a-day world.

I will give two self-sacrificing instances of my sense of duty. Once the Government of India were anxious to link the Indian rupee with the English pound and the House was evenly divided on the subject. My party of 43 in normal times had dwindled to 32, since 11 of them had threatened to resign if I did not permit them freedom of conscience by voting for the 1/6 instead of 1/4 by which we stood in the interest of India. It was clear that this move was intended to give England preference to the extent of 12½ per cent and, as a part of the same scheme, England obtained direct preference of 10 p.c. her net gain was 22½ per cent to the prejudice of India and to the detriment of her farmers and exporters of raw materials against which England exported her finished goods which she sold 10 p.c. cheaper to India than elsewhere.

This preference was settled at the Ottawa Conference at which a member of our party Mr. Shanmukham Chetty was selected by the Government as India's delegate. This agreement was subject to approval by the Assembly. On sounding the members of my party I found that farmers were for preference and those against it were lukewarmly so not because they were against the deal but rather because they distrusted the Government. As I found that the agreement would go through unconditionally I made it conditional for a fixed period of five years, its further extension being subject to the approval of the Assembly. This was agreed to and on its expiry after 5 years its extension was voted by the Assembly. But the currency-link remains and has greatly prejudiced India in the Second Great War as its absence had profited India in the First Great War when the Sovereign was sold in the market for 7/8/- and at one time it fell below it.

From the moment I entered the Assembly I was convinced that the so-called Government of India was no Government at all, but was in reality a mere department of the British administration carried on wholly and entirely for the benefit of Great Britain and its commercial magnates who were jealous of the growing national desire to use up as far as possible India's raw materials locally by starting and developing her own industries, the more so because her alarming growth of population could not be fed upon grass alone but needed a world-market to meet her growing wants. The mechanization of all her industries and the state-piloting of her new industries was insisted upon by the elected members with whom even he nominated non-official Indians were covertly in agreement. That the British Industries needed protection to hold their own even in the Empire markets was a clear proof that the British industries were not able to hold their own in an open market against the throttling competition of Germany, Italy, America and Japan. It was clear from the statistics which showed that Japan was fast driving Lancashire even out of her protected markets and that the textile industry of Lancashire was doomed. I pleaded for the protection of Indian industries pointing out that we were no longer in competition with England, and as this was true, the Government set us free to fight Japan and in some few selected industries gave us protection.

But my policy in entering the Assembly was to force the hands of the Goverment to establish a Control Board of trade to pilot new and protect old industries : In one word, to make India self-supporting country which the Government opposed, no doubt because such a policy would have seriously affected England. That this was obvious permitted no doubt, but the Government of India though all the time pulling for England had all the time to show us a turn that their policy was solely in the interest of India, which at times made their spokesmen despicably insincere and evasive. Any one who cares to go through the pages of the Assembly debates will not fail to find the Government apologists often placed between two stools, one the Secretary of State and another the Assembly and the massive strength of its opinion in spite of the blandishments of official whips.

The Legislative Assembly in which we served was one of the rarest constitutional curious created by the Act of 1919. For while we had a clear majority therein of elected members the statute provided for the rule of the minority officials over the majority. That majority was at times farcical because behind the back of its leaders members were only too easily reduced to support the power that had in the hallow of its hand all the patronage and it is a lure to all people everywhere.

At the present moment when I am penning these lines the future of my country is unpredictable but should it achieve any measure of real responsibility, that responsibility will not be real unless the dispensation of patronage is not made as free as possible from the taint of sycophancy and subserviency not wholly absent in such a democratic country as England where, curiously, the entire judiciary is controlled by a party man, the Lord Chancellor and where all prize appointments are made in return for party services.

I hope this evil practice will not be copied in India.

CHAPTER VII

I AND MY FAMILY

FROM the short account I have given of my parents and their family it will be seen that I am since the death of my brother Adhar in 1915 the sole surviving member of my family the dissolution of which has deprived me of a solace and a comfort which nothing has atoned for.

On my return from England in 1892 and on my appointment as an E.A.C. I naturally began to feel uneasy about my loneliness and I wrote to one or two casual friends in Saugor to find me a companion. They wrote what should have been only too obvious to me that all girls in my caste were married before they reached the age of 12. One such girl might be found if I could not mind marrying a child, which I refused to do because what I wanted was a companion and a partner, not a pet. Marriage within the caste being out of the question, I next thought of marrying an English girl, and my brother had once in a casual talk suggested it as my only chance. He reminded me of his early marriage and lifelong loneliness. He was married when he was 16 and his wife was then 11 drawn from a farmer's family at M. Tatarwada, a village not far from M. Mohari where my elder sister Lilawati was married. On her marriage this girl was baptised Ladli Bahu. She was swarthy and quite a good cook, but in no way companionable to my brother or to me with the result that we treated her as a housekeeper and my brother gave her a fixed sum of money every month to run the household which she did fairly well; but as my brother would not increase her allowance upon the increase of her commitments, as when my father, elder brother and myself, began to live with him, she naturally resented our presence and her own impecuniosity of which

Dr. [illegible] with his daughters – Mrs. Prem K. [illegible], Mrs. Dorothy [illegible], Mrs. [illegible] K. [illegible] and Mrs. Ruby [illegible]

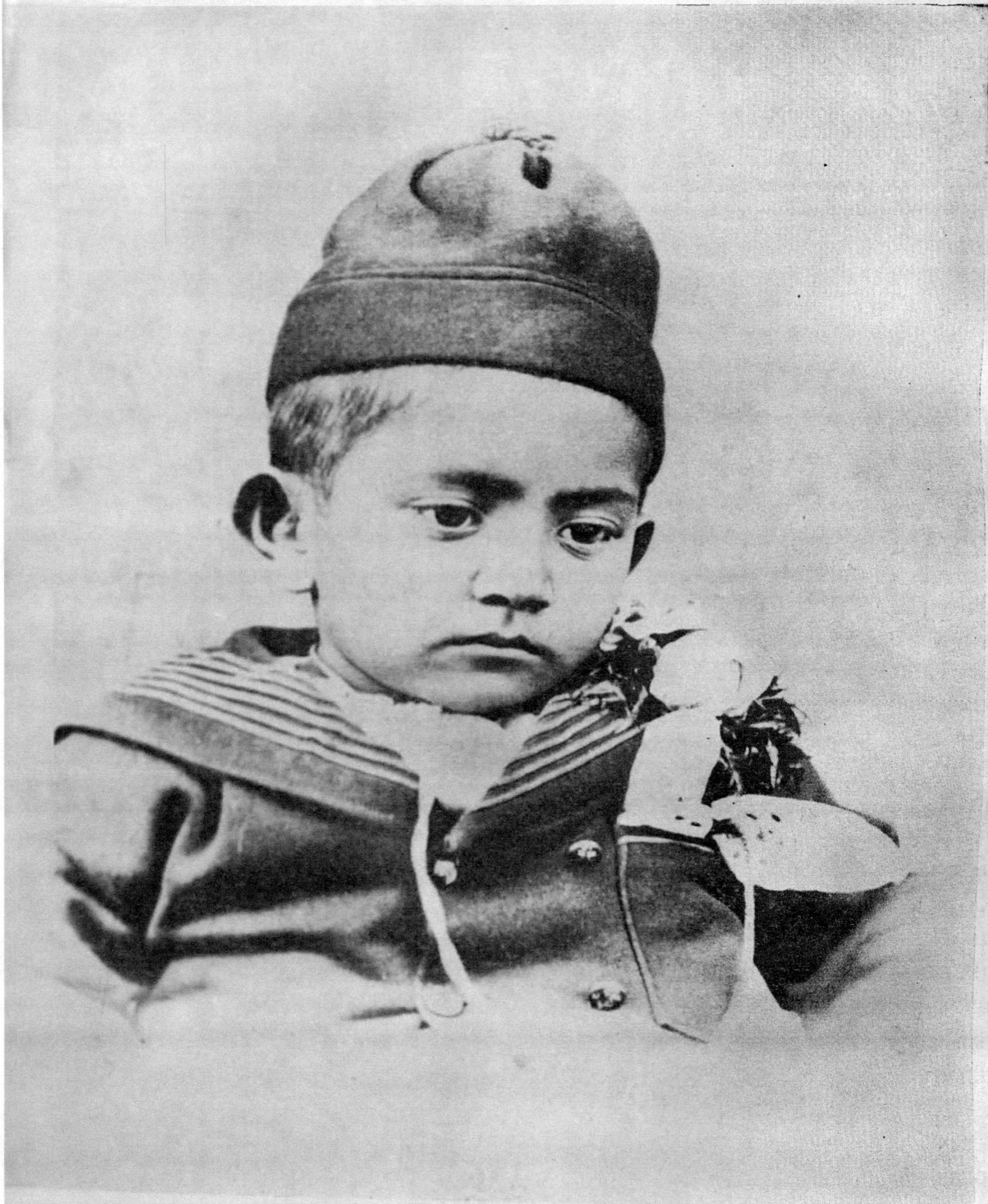

An early portrait of Ernest Gour (Mohan Singh Gour), the only son of Dr. Gour who met an untimely death in 1944

my brother did nothing to relieve her.

But all three of us had nowhere to go, and so we continued to stay on in a house where we were veritable deadheads of which we required no reminder to recall at our meals. My mother who had a shrewd insight into human affairs had always resisted any attempt to decoy her to join our company and so save the Rs. 10/- p.m. that my brother sent her. Though living alone in a big house with innumerable ill-planned rooms many of them threatening to come down any moment, and the most so the one room in which my mother cooked and slept she preferred to haunt like a ghost in her ancestral labyrinth, friendless and neglected with her husband and two sons in Jabalpur, one son in England and her two daughters married and existing with their country clouts in two small villages, Mohari and Chilpahadi and wearing out their youth and strength in grinding corn and cooking meals for their respective cowboys and ploughmen—numbering about a dozen.

My dear sisters once recounted to me their daily drudgery. They commenced the day's work at 3 a.m. when they started grinding 8 seers of *Jowar* or Kodo and 3 seers of wheat, the one for the menials and the other for the household. They had to grind both bulk and fine, and by 5 start making chappaties for the menials who not only ate but took away with them chappaties for their midday meal. This done, my sisters adjusted their toilette and bathed in cold water, summer or winter, after which the household hearth was lighted to cook the family meal for a family of six or eight which took them the whole morning and a part of the afternoon, after which they were to eat their own breakfast-cum-dinner mostly from the offals left on their plates by the male-folk. And there was the mother-in-law to supervise the household and torture my sister by ironical gibes like these : "Beti, you haven't come here to teach the Ramayan—you have come to cook and play the rustic as we all are", which was not an irony but a naked truth to which my sisters with all our poverty and want were complete strangers. And as my brother was holding a government post these women thought that he must be taking plenty of bribes and that therefore all of us including our sisters were living in luxury of which they expected a share which they took by depriving my sisters of the few silver and gold ornaments that our father had with difficulty made for them as their precious hairlooms, which all told could not be worth more than a hundred rupees.

Such was the life to which my orthodox though ignorant father had consigned two of the brightest jewels of our family and my life.

As I have said before my elder sister was hardier and after years of suffering and tutelage accommodated herself to her new environments, though she died of an enlarged spleen at the early age of 40 while my younger sister Mohan Bai died only when she was say 16 of cholera which she had contracted and on which she managed to run home to die. These were tragic episodes in my life, specially the death of my younger sister who was so pretty and at the same time so clever, both of which were treated by her rustic people as serious impediments to hard menial work.

Judging from the description given to me and the observation made by me there appears to run through the female mentality of the women of my caste living in the highlands of Central India in which Saugor is situate, a strong dash of sadism which the men-folk have imbibed though not to the same extent as the women who vie with one another in piling upon the young new-comer all their arduous duties regardless of the capacity of the unfortunate new-comer. The families my two sisters were married into were those of the Malguzars and their own husbands were active members of the household. I visited them both when I went to fetch my sisters on the occasions of some Hindu festivals like the Holi or Diwali.

My sister at Mohari lived in a low tiled shed and I was given a bed in the *Devdhi* or the entrance corridor through which men and beast constantly passed. The only saving grace in my favour was a *Chabutra* or a platform which rose about three feet above the common passage. The cot I was given was called a *pallang* because it was woven with tape and I may add it was luckily free from bugs or other vermin though being devoid of a mosquito-curtain, a prime necessity in all better class beds, I had to dodge between suffocation under my cover and hand-fan which offered no effective or lasting hindrance to a mosquito. On one of my visits, which might be treated as typical of the rest, I reached the village on a pony which my mother had hired for me from a neighbour for one rupee and feed. Our family barber accompanied me. Mohari is, as stated before, 30 miles north of Saugor and lies on a cart-road to Shahpur and Lalitpur. If motors had then been invented and I could afford it would be just about an hour's run. But I took two days and two nights, since starting at 5 a.m. we stopped *en route* for breakfast and rest and my barber companion needed rest as he was on foot and occasionally whipped the horse for me to make it cover 10 miles by noon. We started again at 2 for our first stage where we were welcomed by one of our well-to-do casteman who returned our hospitality that had often enjoyed in his frequent visits to Saugor in some cases in which he was interested. I still remember Bihari Lal as he did all he could to make me comfortable.

He even lent me his own pony to reach Mohari, which I did the next day by 4 P.M. All male members of the household were in the fields, but one or two boys who were playing in the street carried the message of my arrival to the seraglio who sent me a cot and a guilt which some one led me to the *Chabutra* where I waited for the return of my brother-in-law's elder brother who ran my sister's branch of the family. Common usage prohibited the meeting of one's sister's husband as to do so would be accounted lewd—such are the laws and behest of the sanctimonious caste, with the result that my brother in-law Mohan Singh, aged 20, fought shy of me, and I of him during my 36 hours' stay at Mohari. I met Thakur Raghubir Singh Padihar, the doyen of the Malguzar family, aged 70, a fine six-footer, fair, straight and alert who was respected in the neighbourhood for his ability and learning. He took me in hand, and like a kitten on his side, he showed me all the family-fields then sown with wheat. It was mid-February. He then installed me on a padded seat round which I saw a large gathering of men (no women, young or old) who had presumably received the pass-word that I was to read them Ramayan from the old Thakur's book a rare compliment. The Thakur brought this book himself, and opened a page for me to read, which I did in the mock intonation of the Pandit's which all present audibly admired in their whispered applause. I then explained to them in their own language the meaning of the verses, and wove up a story round them which the rustics greatly relished, and as a reward they pressed the old Thakur to press me to stay for a few days till I had finished the chapter that I had started to read to them. The Thakur joined them in pressing me to stay but I pretended some pressing engagement, and so I had to go leaving the chapter unfinished, but as compromise I agreed to read to them two hours in the morning and two in the evening the next day, which the audience greatly relished. They in fact declared a general holiday in honour of my visit which greatly pleased my sister who whispered to me while serving my food that the Zenana were feeling bitter about having to feed the ploughmen without work, but all the same my sister felt very proud and elated to becoming the heroine of the village whose women idolised her as the elder sister of the reader of Ramayan.

The secret of my popularity lay in my free translation into Bundelkhandi dialect the sacred verses in high flown Hindi of Mathura. In next day my sister was given a fine horse to take her home and we left Mohari at 5 A.M. on the third day of my arrival, and several villagers accompanied us for a few paces to make their farewell. A month later the village Patwari happened to meet me in Saugor and on my inviting him to dinner he confided to me that my reading of the Ramayan was much appreciated as the old Thakur read the verses but never explained them to the people as he considered such course as blasphemy.

I had once or twice paid a visit to Chil Pahadi where my younger sister was married and there too the doyen of the family received and escorted me and all I saw of my brother-in-law was a glimpse one morning at 8 when he was basking in the sun and struggling with his illiteracy at the age of 10 by learning the alphabet at the hands of the family priest. He looked to me a tall fair boy with light blue eyes as are many boys and girls of my caste who have for generations lived and died in the uplands of Bundelkhand.

In strange contrast to my own people the three girls whom my two brothers and Nephew Murli Manohar married were dark though passable and their children were likewise common.

When on my return from England I was anxious to get married I had planned a marriage in the caste of which I was proud, but as I could not get a girl of any age above 10 or 11, I chanced to meet a Dr. Baldeo Singh who had then just retired from a subordinate medical post he had held in Nagpur. He had built a big bungalow in Bhandara where he had acquired a fair practice to which he added the job of selling drugs of which he used to import a consignment from England and which being fresh and undiluted commanded a ready sale amongst the Indian officials who were thereby driven to receive his treatment. As such, he also became my doctor, and one of the E.A.Cs, Mr. Trimbak Nilkanth Deshmukh who used to spend some time every evening at mine suggested that if I wanted to marry in the caste, Dr. Baldeo had three daughters, pretty, educated and of course of a suitable age. He seems to have opened the topic to the doctor for he told me that the doctor who was a convert would not like any of his children to be married to a heathen. Of his five children, one son and four daughters, two had already been married, the oldest, a daughter to a Sub Post-Master who had retired and his son Maksudan, a never do-well, to a girl of whose parents I have no inkling. He passed through life as a dependent of his sister Helen who never married but was a Sub-Assistant Surgeon at Bundi where she died. Her next sister by Olivia was married to me. She too died on the 28th March 1941. Her youngest sister Ada was married to a man who worked in a Mission. She died only a couple of years after her marriage. Upon first meeting Olivia I was informed that she was engaged to be married to a Mr. Ghose, a teacher in a Missionary school at Allahabad. Her father, Baldeo Ram Singh, told me in confidence that I should not marry her, as she was not good enough for me and was well fitted for a school-master like Ghose to whom she was practically engaged. I must say that her father's advice was sound and I was unhappy from the very date of my marriage, though for appearance sake I endured her for a period of 49 years (1893-1941). As she is now dead I shall not go into further details beyond adding that mine was the vicious case of marry in haste and repent at leisure though I never had any leisure for it.

By her I became the father of ten children, two sons and eight daughters. Of these a son and two daughters died within a year or two of their birth, two daughters were taken off in their twenties. The four daughters now alive are all well married and three of them are graduates and well able to look after themselves, but not so the son who has done nothing at school or in life and has moreover from early age shown a longing for menial company and drink which I have failed to correct. After years of study and observation I am firmly convinced that human character as much as animal character closely follows the course of heredity and evil impulses more than virtuous trails are like weeds easy of transmission. As it is I am last of the Gours to possess such spark of genius as might still linger in our family.

CHAPTER VIII

I AND MY PEOPLE

HAVING travelled over most part of the world and come into contact with all and sundry from the highest to the lowest in the scale of life, I feel that of all people I have met none can be compared to my people in India, who have acquired habits of thought and action all their own, and which will not bear the remotest comparison with any nation on the surface of the globe. For one thing, no other country in the world has that unique institution of caste. They have guilds and classes, division of the people into sections, but they are not ordained and immutable clinging to the man throughout life independently of his trade, occupation or calling and confining him to the narrow shell of his caste and placing upon him duties and obligations which he is not free to discard or disregard. If he dare he is put out of the caste and thereupon subjected to caste ostracism and treated as an enemy of the caste.

In modern times, and the more so in recent years, this draconian courage has become relaxed with the growth of western education and the commingling of the caste by a freer recourse to the trade or profession, while I happen to have undermind its solidarity by my Act permitting intermarriages (inter-alia) between all castes without incurring any of their penalties, but the innate conservation of people has confined the scope of this measure within narrow limits limiting it into practice to the educated members of the middle classes and a few others who had been chafing at the invidious distinctions it made between the twice-born and the Shudras.

But this Act was only passed in 1923 and I had lived in an era in which caste had supernatural origin and sanction. From early life to the age of 16 I was myself one of its rigid adherents and cooked my own meal while at school in Jabalpur, but the daily ordeal of lighting wet wood and digesting half-cooked meals relaxed my ritual observance of its iron discipline till my release ripened into a revolt and a vocal crusade against its irrationality and inhumanity. This feeling was intensified by the fate of my two sisters and the lesson it pointed to me, with the result that on my return from England I became anxious to secure power to reform my people and make their lives cleaner, healthier and happier than is possible under the routinism of caste. The first thing that I had planed to do was to unite and unify my people, by removing their fissiperous habits and thought. In my judgment communalism, racialism and nationalism are all the outcome of the narrow conception of self which all religions, Buddhism only excepted, postulate. Buddhism scotches that conception, and widens the field to all sentient life. I studied Buddhism and its deep philosophy and published my researches in a work called "The spirit of Buddhism." I invoked the aid of legislature in ameliorating the law of succession which prescribes Hindu women inheriting their near and dear relations property. I gave them liberty to live away from their husbands if they were ill-treated, and above all neglected. I have given details of the measures I was able to pass thereabout. But with all that the reforms effected so far have not even cracked the crust of orthodoxy and those who wish to retain its support must demonstrailly observe its vagaries. Those who cannot, but yet wish to retain its favour, have entered into a spontaneous compromise with themselves in that they observe the tenets of both. While in a mixed company they don European clothes and eat at table and have furnished a room for two in the European style. But when they are by themselves or with their Hindu dualists they eat on the ground having their body and on all festive and funeral occasions they follow the rigours of the caste. The orthodox, finding themselves following a lost cause, have advanced a step of two to meet them. But this is not true of all regions. For instance, in my caste, that of the Rajputs, I did not find many examples of this intermediate obedience ; while my brother Dr. Adhar Singh who set my pace in social observance had openly and aggressively out-casted his caste, which I did too, though living as I was in the midst of a people not one of whom belonged to my caste I was out of their contact and so out of their thoughts. As such my battle of life has been unaided by any one, a near or distant relations, a member of my caste or tribe. On the other hand I had all along to face the full volley of overt and covert attacks or antipathy from the other more advanced and better organized communities and castes. Many men in my position would have contrived to place themselves under the sheltering wing of Government as I know many have done and have risen to the topmost rung of the official leader, but I don't suppose to have been born or equipped for such success, and from early life my resolve to speak the truth, the whole truth and nothing but the truth, a thing every witness is supposed to do, clung to me and this trait in my character has been the subject of comment in several published works about India. I came across one quotation quite casually and till I lighted upon it I had never heard of the book or its author, though he was at one time editor of the Civil and Military Gazettee, and as such has *throughout* his book followed the anti-Indian policy of an average Englishman living in his own narrow circle, with no concern or contact with a "Damned Nigger'' like myself. This gentleman appears to have been on the press but on the Simon Cammission to which he gives considerable space in his work, "Stark India", so called because he professes to portray it stark naked as he found it. On p. 182 he gives a sketchy pen-picture of some Indians whom he singles out as outstanding personalities of the country and including me among them he jerks out the few following words: "Sir Hari Singh Gour, a legal lion with razor-like mind and rapier like tongue''.

Several official members of the Assembly have commented upon my downright straight-forwardness but I am not here to relate to the reader my collected chits, trying to show why, since I was only my status and my position in the Indian society is that of a rank outsider, and that as such I comment upon its construction and composition. One thing I have noticed which seems to be common to both British and Indian members of the Bar that while fellow professionals in all other professions became combined and formed a kind of trade union for mutual help, I have found no such contact between members of the legal profession. While in India I tried to create one. It was short—lived. In England I have nominally practised in the Privy Council for a period of five years during which I have come in contact with many members of my profession, both on the Bench and the Bar but I have noticed tbe same apathy as I marked in India, where a close latent sympathy permeates certain advanced classes of Hindus, *e.g.* the Bengalis, the Maratha Brahmin, the Kayasthas, the South Indian about whom I wish to speak with who reserve. But these are not all the cliques but only some of them. The Moslems naturally fall upon one another, and so do the other small communities like the Parsis whose comaradie is proverbial; and so is that of the Marwaris regardless of caste. These and a thousand other cliques divide and disrupt the people who have become congenitally incompetent to unit with other people.

This stern isolationism of Hinduism follows its religious doctrine of aloofness. No other religion in the world has inculcated such monstrous rise. Gautam Buddha rose against the priestly cult of divide and rule and he gave us a doctrine that uplifted man from the beast that he was and is to an angel and his creed submerged Hinduism for a thousand years, after which the old contemptibles lying in wait saw their chance, and made a deadly dash upon the creed of human brotherhood and revived their old stunt by performing a horse-sacrifice. The banishment of Buddhism from India marks the sorriest page in human soiety. Old castes reappeared, not in fours but in thousands, which the Census Commissioner now completes as 3,5000. Though Hinduism has expelled Buddhism from the land of its birth, Hinduism has not thereby secured its archaic monopoly, and more modern religions, Christianity and Islam, have levelled their attack upon an inhuman creed and wrested from it no less than a hundred million adherents. And as education grows and reaches the masses, Hinduism will die a much belated death and will remain a mere name in the multitudious castes and creeds into which it is resolving itself. Chief amongst them are already Sikhism, the Arya Samaj, the Brahma Samaj and many more of which the names are legions.

I have tried to reform Hinduism, but now see that it is past reformation, though I still feel that whatever my people may drift into, they will still remain Hindus in name if they do not become openly converted to another non-Aryan religion conversion into which shall postulate their annihilation.

Hinduism in India has become a militant creed like what it was in the days of the Prophet and Hindu converts are as usual more aggressively anti-Hindu than Hindu heretics belonging to an allied creed. In political life India is mobilising itself for her independence. I devoutly hope and pray that it will attain it with the aids and force of international cooperation. But before it effectively achieves it, it will not fail to realise that her long thousand years of ignomy and servitude was due to its religion and that it can never realise its independence unless it escapes from the thraldom of caste and religion and develops a mentality that treats religion, caste and communalism as both anti-national and anti-moral.

But this is my hope for the future. In my long years I have constantly suffered from the secret and subtle influences of my own countrymen, who have poisoned the ears of those in authority by recounting to them my defects, some real and most of them imaginary.

For example, there was a time when I was naturally anxious to obtain power that might enable me to cleanse my people from the augean stables of superstition and servitude. But the very people whom I wished to cleanse joined hands to defeat me. I shall give an example. I was a member of the Legislative Assembly from 1921-1935 and for much of that time leader of the opposition. As such, I was in close contact with the three Indian members of the Viceroy's Council, which in the first years of my membership had Sir Tej Bahadur Sapru, Sir Mian Mohamed Shafi and Sir Bhupendra Nath Mitra, two of whom belonged to my profession. and thus knew and respected me on account of my published legal works. It was usual in those days, as it is now, for the local Government to send a confidential docket of every member elected or nominated to the Legislative Assembly which served as a "who's who" of such member to members of the Government of India. My Government had presumably given me a docket, the character of which I am free to guess from the following facts. Sir Frank Sly was the First Governor of the Province appointed under the Act of 1919. Long before he took office in 1921, he had known me while he served as Political Agent Chhattisgarh Feudatories and as the Commissioner of Nagpur which he was during the Great War and in 1918 when Mr. Montague visited India. As I have stated before I had identified myself with the zamindars of Chhattisgarh and had appeared for them before the Privy Council in 1911. In 1918 on close of the war there was a vacancy in the Presidentship of the Nagpur Municipality till then held by a nominee of Government who had been again and again re-elected as a matter of course with no opposition for several trienniums. This time I opposed him not at a spur of any party but on my own just to secure power to enable me to modernise Nagpur which was till then as it is still one of the by-words for dirt and squalor, dust and dearth of water during the dry season, and yet it was boosted as the Capital of two joint Provinces of the C.P. and Berar. My predecessor was a very wealthy landlord, but his idea of health and sanitation might be judged from the fact that he lived in his ancestral house which faced the burning ghat and was backed by an open latrine.

The Municipality consisted of 40 members of whom only about 32 were elected, eight were nominated and even out of 32 as many were "Jee-hazurs" of Government. I canvassed and as usual about 35 out of the lot promised me their votes. But on the fateful day I secured 21 votes against my opponent's 18, one an Anglo-Indian E.A.C. remained neutral. I was elected, much to the disgust of Mr. Sly, and as I lost no time in launching my scheme for the daming of Kanhan, a river 10 miles from Nagpur, and the reshaping of Nagpur according to the report of Prof. Geddes whom I had invited to speak to my fellow citizens on the necessity of town-planning, I asphalted some of the roads, cemented others and made the public realize that we were their servants and not their masters which they greatly appreciated. The great mysterious world-wide "fever" visited Nagpur, but I distributed two lac bottles of germicidal liquid, the basic ingredient was the essence of ainesac (Ajwain), which reduced mortality in Nagpur to an extent noted by the Government of India who described my prophylactic as talismanic in its effect. The C.P. Government congratulated me upon my self-sacrificing service, in organizing a thoroughly effective relief which reduced mortality in Nagpur by far and away of the lowest in India. The mortality of Nagpur was about 1.8 p.c. during the apex of the epidemic againt 2.9 of another place described as practically immune from the scourge.

However, as I had drafted and presented a note on the Indian Reforms as head of the Graduates' Association which reminded Mr. Montague of his Government's Committment of the 16th April 1917 and which, I added, could not be forgotten as it was for several million pounds worth of consideration paid, I pointed out that it is easier to blend oil with water than combine centralised bureaucracy with even the thin end of democracy, which was intended to condemn Lionel Curtis's scheme of Dyarchy which the Act of 1919 had introduced and the incongruity of which became soon apparent.

Mr. Montague as the Secretary for India had installed a curious machinery of Government in which elected majority itself rumpled as much as they liked but they had no status and in fact no option. The constitution was in fact an op n fa ce, and the Congress were not boycotting it. I was driven into it with the hope of improving some of the laws which in my opinion had long cried out for reform and some of which I was able to amend and alter though I could have gone too faster if I were in power, which I never had because of the dual diffidence in my policy. Th Gov rnment looked upon me as an extremist and the Congress as an extreme moderate with the result that both sides treated me as u reliable, which in a sense I was, because I was never a tool an would never become one in the hands of either party, both of which regarded me as selfish and unscrupulous and as not in the remotest sense public-spirited or patriotic.

(Pages missing)

GOD AND THE UNIVERSE

[These pieces were probably intended to form the last Chapter of the autobiography though the first of them is taken from an article 'Science's Survey of the Universe' and the others are elaborations of similar material elsewhere. They contain Dr. Gour's established views on Religion, and would necessarily form part of a chapter : 'My Religion'.

—Editors]

BOTH the scientists and the laymen have been anxious to ascertain if the scheme of the universe affords any evidence of the presence of God as the Almighty personal or impersonal force guiding and controlling it. The usual argument that God created man and rules over him, and visits his acts with rewards and punishment, is falsified by the story of his creation; the other argument that the entire universe follows his will in an orderly movement is equally exploded by science. There remains the question of the beginning and ending of the universe upon which science is more cautious. For while it is able to assert that the cosmos came into being and is proceeding to its end, it is not able to say how it really began though it is able to assert how it will really end. From the foregoing account it will be seen that all the universe is empty except for small dots floating through in the form of nabulae and stellar galaxies or constellations which make its emptiness look even more emptier and these are composed of limited elements found on the earth and which on analysis are composed of atoms with protons and electrons revolving round them. There are again corpuscles or waves of energy the material of which has taken form within limits beyond which it passes out of the range of matter and science has to invent the pretence of a material medium called ether in Universe, which is but a mathematical postulate, and of whose presence there is no tangible evidence. At this stage the physics reaches the verge of metaphysics and metaphysics meanders through a maze of theories and counterof gods, demons, angels, satans, the wizard and miracle man and to a people who believed in ghosts and Satyas as barefacedly intermingling with man as Haris Babu jostling through the *maidan* of Calcutta, no social reformer like Buddha or Christ could command a following unless he carried his head in a halo of celestial crown and it must be said to the credit of Sakyamuni that inspite of numerous man-gods all over and his own disciples thrusting upon him the honour of deification Buddha resented such superstitions and venerations as unworthy of them as his desciples. But the scriptures speak differently of the protagonists of other religions. As for *Karma* and reincarnation the following hiata seem to stand in the way of Karma. In order that a person should be rewarded or punished for his deeds, there must be a judge to decide and the survival of consciousness to recognise the sanction to a uniform standard to decide upon which is postulated in reincarnation but without support, but on the contrary with some scientific *contratemp*. Further, if reincarnation is the resultant penalty for one's craving and sin, how is it reconcilable with *maya* to which it is antithical ? Lastly the Hindu-cum-Buddhist view of life that it is painful is true. Its pleasures are meagre and few while its sorrows are constant and numerous. Hinduism solved the problem by self-retreat so that the body got inured to its travails; otherwise it practised isolation and seclusion and a life of lonely individualism. Buddhism modified this severity by practising the role of self-control and self-sacrifice and finally self-effacement. Buddha did not eschew human society but on the other hand inculcated human service which he made the keynote of his teaching. He has seen the duel pains of Nature as of Man, those of Nature—sickness, old age, disease and death—those of man—jealousy, revenge, blood-feud, vendetta, hunger, penury, want—and the Hindu remedy for both was sheer defeatism while Buddha's was an effective fight by employment of human resources and human brotherhood. Its result will be found writ large in the glorious pages of Buddhist India (600 B.C.—750 A.D.). As for Christianity it had to pass through ages of strife and struggle and it has been truly said that the Church of Christ has been built with the blood of its martyrs. In the end the two religions are both philanthropic and their reconciliation and theories none of which has so far attained the stage of reasonable certainties. It is in this cloud-land of uncertainties and conjecture that they walk in to illumine the darkness with its appeal to the revelation against which science can only shake its head. The fact is that science is at present unable to assert though it can safely deny the truth of revelation but the only verdict it is able to give is not that of true or false, but one of "not proven."

Science is convinced that there is no accuracy or precision in nature and that its erratic course may be compared to that of a river as compared with that of a canal running alongside of it. In all its acts, it is wanton, wasteful and chimerical. Our life has come into existence and our planet has attained its requisite density, temperature and condition, as the first fruit of its condensation and reduction to ash and dust the vital atomy of radioactivity. Our age is cast in a dying universe, one that has entered in final stage of dissolution by the radiation of its vital energy into the cold space of the cosmos where the temperature must be some 4 degrees above the absolute zero, about 484°F degree below the freezing point and even lower in the vast stretches of space that lie out of the range of stellar radiation.

Taking life on the earth we see how its latitude is ill-adapted to the growth of flora and fauna which was to fight its climatic and numerous other aberrations. The planet was not therefore made the receptacle of life, but life somehow came into existence inspite of its drawbacks.

That life is purely mechanical and is becoming increasingly established. Its creation by an author is having increasingly disproved. The 20th century has reconciled the conflict between the two rival theories of the 19th century—that light was corpuscular and that it was not corpuscular but merely undulatory. The fact, now found, is that it is both at the same time, or to be more correct, the corpuscles and waves are in essence the same thing.

The language of a Scripture is necessarily topical. In an age ment in the spiritual life by a God or his vicegerent on earth, but in one word *Nirvan,* which he used to mean mental rest free from desire and its attendant suffering. The term *Nirvan* is added by Buddha for the resulting happiness from good deeds evidencing self-descipline, self-control, self-sacrifice and finally self-effacement. The term is formed out of *Nirvan* to blow, that is to blow out one's selfishness from thought, acts and deeds. But this limited human reaction did not appeal to the disciples who wanted some return higher and deeper than a mental beautitude which as a part of the sensual mirage of *Maya* was itself a transient illusion. The word had to be exalted to something heavenly, something divine to compete with the oriental imagery of spiritual beautitude which it merged and into which it so remains in most of its schools, where it has reached the sense of salvation. Similarly the term *Karma* though deep-rooted in Hindu Philosophy, appears to have received expanding sense in Buddhism from its pristine sense of deed which received appropriate sanction in the intaglio of the world to destiny which moulded the future life. The term was probably coined not only to evade a closer search for the mystery of life and death, but also as an incentive for good deeds. But to a modern rationalist, *Karma* has not only no justification and no sense in the ever passing local and transient regimen of morality—a man's earthly deeds, right or wrong according to earthly standards cannot be the avenue to another life in which virtue and sin are to be as effemereal as in this life.

Buddha's teaching was mainly secular, though out of respect to his desciples he had adopted the Hindu etiology of life, *i.e.*, the doctrine of reincarnation or succession of lives resulting from the mental craving for life, higher or lower, according to one's deeds or '*Karma*'. This simple but in the result all energy-devouring dogma has become rooted in lands outside the ambit of Hinduism, *e.g.*, the Persia and the other Moslem countries. In his first sermon preached at Sarnath *cum* Benares Buddha preached the root-cause of human suffering to be human craving or desire for freedom from poverty and want and other wants and wishes too numerous and varied to categorise and the only sedative to such want is self-sacrifice, if not union would realize the dream of the world-planner for a real world-religion.

The Aryans were divided into a fighting clan, accompanied by their priests on the one hand and merchants and menials on the other. These four classes, at one time occupational, had already become crystallized into set castes, the two brightests of whom had already started a bitter struggle for the social supremacy of their own caste. The Brahmins had at first yielded to the Rajputs, but subtlely relegated them to fighting and rule subject to their spiritual authority which was yet unconceded by those who had made notable contribution to the scriptures of the Hindi hegemony, the fact being that when Buddha was born India was in a state of political, religious, racial and social chaos. When Buddha grew up, his reflective mind realised the ultimate tendency of this confusion. He sought to remedy it. By the dual process of mental elimination and synthesis he found that all the struggles and sufferings of life are due the possession of self. Self, self, self pervaded the universe, and his main purpose was to control if he could not resolve this self. He had found it done by religious recluses who had withdrawn from the world and ended their lives aloof from the ambitious drives and despondent struggles of the common people. He had evidence of the futility of wealth and power and so renounced both. He saw for himself the transitoriness of life and so provided against its attendant misery. His one purpose in life was to make human life easier and better, but his teaching was too refined and exalted. All of it was contained in his two precepts, called the four Noble truths and the Eight-fold Path to reach them. The one is fundamental, the other personal. The truths are : (1) life is pain (2) its cause is desire (3) and its cure is its cessation (4) achieved by right feeling, right action, right timing, right effort, right recollectedness and right meditation. In short the evil of life can only be subdued by good thought and action for which there is neither heaven or hell, reward or punish-

Absolute *i.e.*, the ultimate stratum beyond which nothing remains. In the Hindu view the sensual world is merely phenomenal called *Maya* (a mirage, an illusion). Such is life and all that appertains to it. It is a ripple disturbing the tranquility and calm of the ocean. As a disturbance it is an evil, but life follows life in succession as one ripple follows another created by the same wind. When the soul is finally released from the mortal bondage is reabsorbed by Brahma, the Be all and the End all of all cosmic creation.

Into this Brahma, the Universal Soul, the land of bliss, the emancipated spirit sits cross-legged on the calix of a lotus of which the Mahayan cult gives a detailed fancy picture more elaborate than that of the New Jerusalem in the Gospel of St. John (***Sukhavati Sutra***, 33 S. B. E. p. 23). Both the Nirvan and the four noble truths of Sakyamuni are tacitly abandoned in favour of Amitabhava (or, for short Amida) and the five precepts which are the unerring prototypes of the Christian Decalogue and forbid killing, stealing, lying, drinking and debauchery. On a later date (*Lotus Sutra*, about 300 A.D.), a selection of magic spells was added for protection against disease or demons and for the realization of a wish to beget a son or prosperity in business, while in China, a charm can be had for spelling death or other harm to one's enemy.

The Mahayan Buddhism has developed into two main sects of Shin and Zen in Japan, the one depending on faith, the other more aristocratic on meditation which after ten or twenty years creates the flash of mental illumination corresponding to the flash of enlightenment that came to the Sakyamuni after meditation under the Bo (39 S.B.E. Pt. 2, p. 138). The Shin sect is followed by the masses in Japan where it is one of the closely related "Jodo" sects followed by about two-thirds of the population.

Buddhism both ancient and modern is philosophy with derivative action. Christianity is all action and no philosophy. So is Islam. If the founders of these religions were to return to earth they would be alarmingly surprised to find their simple teachings so grossly magnified and mutilated. But no religion can stand the test of time without permutation and combination to make it acceptable to the people whose cravings are as varied as are the customs and habits self-effacement and it is the master note in original Buddhism. But no religion remains as it is first conceived, and such has been the history of both Buddhism and Christianity which started with the Sermon on the Mount closely allied to and believed to be inspired by Buddha's Sarnath Sermon, with this difference that the good deeds in Christianity were to be rewarded while those in Buddhism were their own reward.

This high ideal was too big a climb for the world of self-seekers and soon after the Master's death plans were formed to amplify and popularise his canon to reconcile with the tenets of Brahiminism, resulting in the emergence of the Mahayan School (the Big Vehicle, about 450 B.C.) which has assumed local variations in countries like China and Japan, while other countries like Ceylon and Burma still remain loyal to primitive Buddhism, and follow the little vehicle (or the Hinyan School).

Human nature is the same all over the world and two seeds planted in two countries would raise trees forming distinct species congenial to the texture of the soil, temperature and climate and other local attributes.

Christianity like Buddhism did not take long to split into two factions of which the apostles are St. John and St. Mathew.

Religion without a God and without a soul to receive reward and punishment and a heaven and a hell in which to receive it is cruder, but the only religion that would mediate to the common people who cannot ascend the mountain-top of metaphysical insight. The founder of Buddhism was, in his own life, faced with these questions, and he was asked about God, the soul and its salvation, but he evaded them by pointing out that these questions were not the essence of his teaching. Buddhism has thus been rightly described as originating with no such appendages of religion which was the essence of Hinduism from which Buddhism was a dissent. Since the Mahayan adopted the ready-made theocracy of Hinduism it called for the Hindu view of God, the soul and the human destiny. So far as God is concerned the Hindu and the Rabbanical views are two things apart: the former's conception of God is impersonal spirit pervading and dominating the univese which may be called the as smoke from the candles of the devout eclipses the face of Virgin Mary. Take an example, faith in the Absolute—as the universal spirit of God cannot survive the presence of evil, crime, injustice and pain in the world and the ferocious battle for survival that every living creature is subjected to. Nor are these facts in consonance with the view of religion that God is the supreme ruler of the universe which as Mr. Bertrand Russel has pointed out "is all spots and jumps, without unity, without continuity, without coherence or orderliness or any of the other properties that governs love. Indeed, there is little but prejudice and habit to be said for the view that there is a world at all." (*Scientific Outlook*, p. 98).

The supreme wisdom of Sakyamuni of avoiding these pitfalls by refusing a peep into the Unknown and Unknowable secrets of the universe was at one time its strength, but in the end has proved to be the death-knell of Buddhism while the contrary assertion of Christ has had the same result, the truth being that man is constituted with very limited mentality and both his curiosity and ambition do not recognize his inherent limitations, which the quacks implement by their own conjectures and conceptions. But if these be ignored the crucial creed of Buddhism and Christianity would be found to be more intimate than the pandits of the two religions would acknowledge. And of the two Buddhism is more modern than Christianity.

23-1-44

of the populace all over the world. No religion can be usefully studied without its background of contemporary life and history of the people and the immediate purpose it was meant to serve. Such was Buddhism founded to unite all India, and through it all mankind in a closer bond of mutual aid and unity. Jesus's mission was confined to the submerged faith of Palestine whom the preacher strove to raise against the combined yoke of Rome and the Rabbi while he preached his gospel as a haloed cry to which all else was accessory.

As such the Christianity of today has neither the identity nor the authenticity of the teaching of Jesus if we can unravel them from the embellishments imparted to it in the course of a century which preparted the crucification and the composition of the Gospels. Even then the Jewish conception of God as a personal being had not disappeared, for St. Paul described Christ as "the image of the unseen God" (Col I—15) and Christ himself is reported as saying, "He that hath seen me hath seen the Father". The abstract conception of God as omniscient and all-pervading creator of the universe escaped the wildest stretch of human imagination.

Modern science has reached the conclusion that all things we see or feel in the universe are composed of radium, but what is radium and what lies behind it science is unable to say, nor is it able to state how and when the universe came into being, though it is able to say that it is now in the process of dissolution, but what will come out of it there-after is equally unknown. In other words, while science is able to probe its present, it is at sea as to its past and future. It leaves this blank to speculation and conjecture, and theologians use it as a corroboration of their revelation, which is a *non-sequitur* but how many people read logic, and how many use their reason. Most of us flourish on sentiment and a fancied ideology which weaves itself tightly into the innermost fibre of our brain till it constructs a new world, a new heaven and a new hell and for ourselves an eternal life.

This is the genesis of the Hindu philosophy which has entangled the pure Rationalism of primitive Buddhism and primitive Christanity, but the intricate embroidery since has as much edified the original faiths

Fascimile of a letter addressed to the editor of the *Orient Post*

MY COLLEGE DAYS

PROF. BREMNER

I received as a shock the news that Prof. Bremner had left the college for good. If I had known that he was going to retire from the college, I should have joined with those who gave him an affectionate farewell. I knew Prof. Bremner from the day when he first landed in Nagpur. Before he arrived the college was a second grade institution known as the Free Church Institution. I well remember the imposing building in which the institution used to meet. Its site is now partially occupied by the Hislop College Hostel. The old building was a massive stony structure fronting the lake with high Corinthian columns adding to its imposing grandeur. It had one large central hall which was at the time, and would if it existed now, be the largest hall in Nagpur. It could not have measured less than 125′ by 60′. There were four big rooms on either side of this hall in which the school and college classes used to meet. The Rev. Mr. Cooper was the Principal of this institution and the other Professors were Messrs. Whitton, Bhagwant Prashad and Sadashiva Jayaram. As soon as the institution was converted into a first grade college, two more European professors were recruited to strengthen the staff and these were Prof. Bremner and the late Rev. Dr. Alexander Robertson. There accompanied Mr. Alexander who was appointed to the Wilson College, Bombay.

I believe all the three landed in Bombay together in May or June about 1887. I well remember the day when the two new Professors arrived. The old practice of the institution was that all students met in the Central Hall and waited the arrival of a bullock cart which brought to the institution Profs. Cooper, Whitton and a third, a Norwegian gentleman, later on replaced by a Scotchman, whose association with the institution, however, was shortlived. We used to stand in the portico of the institution and watch the arrival of this cart driven by two piebald bullocks. The peon of the institution was one Behari, a faithful servant, who lived and died serving the institution. He had in course of time, by reason of his seniority, gained disciplinary power over the students in the absence of the professors. And if the students were inclined to be rowdy before the arrival of the cart, it was Behari who corrected them. He would often threaten the peccant students with pains and penalties of fine, and late payment of his scholarship, and when these were of no avail he would solemnly say that if the peccant student did not behave well, he would lose his books. This ultimatum seldom failed to bring the offending students to their knees. The arrival of the cart was timed 10 O' clock, but then punctuality depended upon the pace of the bullocks and the weather. If it was a rainy day we waited for its arrival till 10-30 and if the cart did not arrive Behari used to declare a holiday, shut the doors of the institution up and the students were free to return to their lodgings. But on ordinary days the cart used to be punctual within a few minutes of its appointed time. As soon as it discharged its professorial hold, the first bell used to be rung out to collect the scattered students into the Hall where prayers were said by one of the European Professors and Mr. Anant Singh who acted as clerk to the Senatus Academicus of the institution. This patriarchal practice of commencing the school life was put a stop to upon its development into a college signalised by the arrival of the two Professors whom I have named. The students were naturally anxious to discuss the features and the qualifications of the new arrivals, and the Rev. Mr. Cooper had informed the students that the two Professors were both distinguished men whom the Home Board had appointed to strengthen the existing staff of the institution upon its emergence as a first grade college. On the morning of the day when the two Professors arrived, we met them in the Hall. Mr. Bremner looked extremely boyish. He was tall and slender but with scarcely any hirsute adornment upon his upper leg. His colleague Dr. Robertson looked a much older man. I was one of the first set of students of the Junior B. A. class at the time, and I had decided to take Honours both in English and Philosophy. Messrs. Whitton and Bremner were selected to teach me these subjects and as I was the only

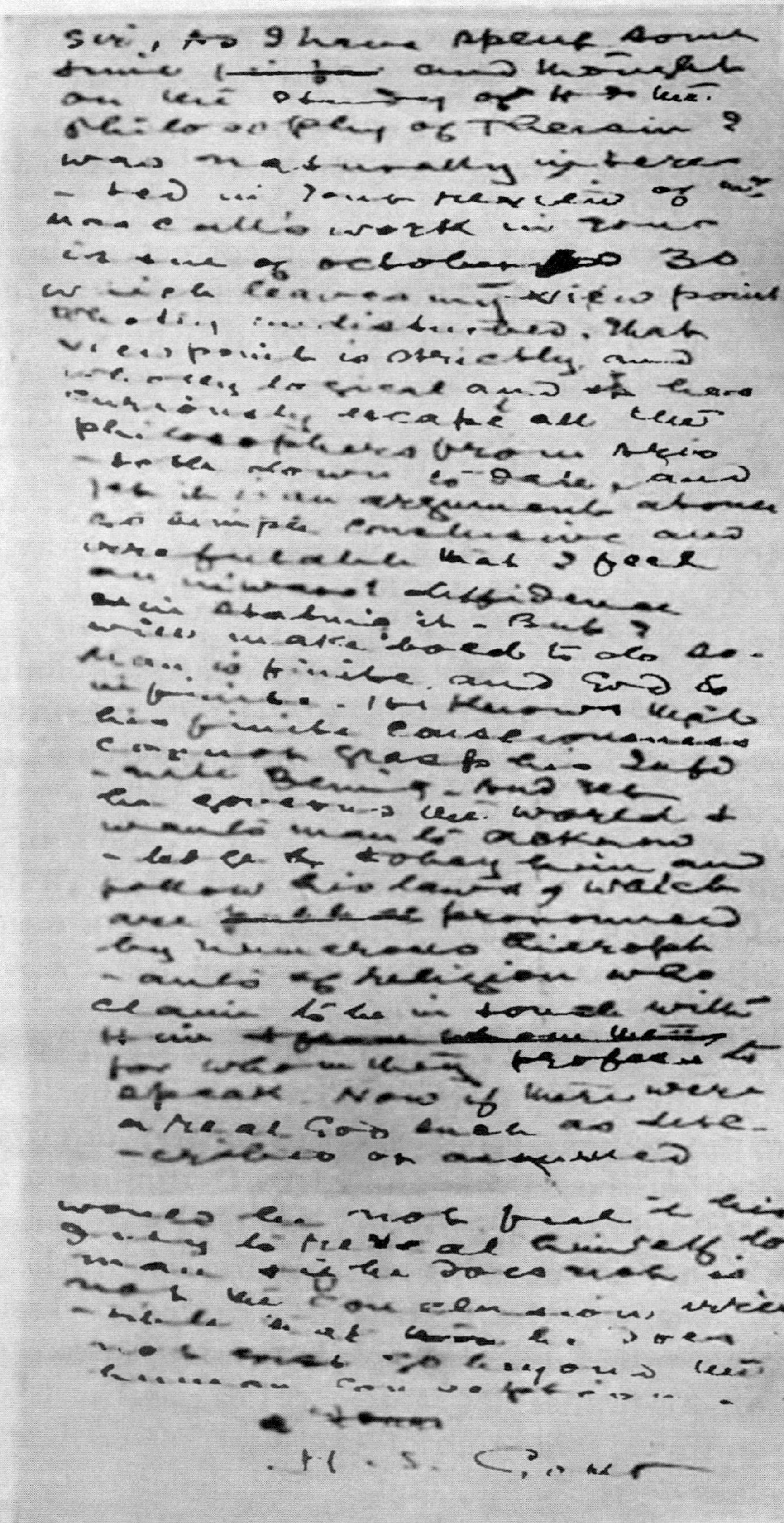

Sir, As I have spent some time and thought on the study of the philosophy of Theism I was naturally interested in your review of Mr. Mascall's work in your issue of October 30 which leaves my view point wholly undisturbed. That view point is strictly and wholly logical and has curiously escaped all the philosophers from Aristotle down to date, and yet it is an argument at once so simple conclusive and irrefutable that I feel an unusual diffidence in stating it. But I will make bold to do so. Man is finite and God is infinite. He knows that his finite consciousness cannot grasp his Infinite Being. And yet he governs the world & wants man to acknowledge him and follow his laws which are pronounced by numerous hierophants of religion who claim to be in touch with Him for whom they profess to speak. Now if there were a real God such as he is credited or assumed would he not feel it his duty to reveal himself to man. If he does not is not the conclusion inevitable that he does not exist beyond the human conception.

Yours

H. S. Gour

Fascimile of a letter written by Dr. Gour to some unidentified journal.

the students. The result was that the mofussal students were seriously handicapped in a competition with the Metropolitan students.

Prof. Bremner taught me Philosophy and English. I had to learn History by myself. He also taught me Political Economy. At the end of March 1889 the suggestion appears to have been made to the Senate of the College that I should be assisted into going to Edinburgh to complete my course for a college degree. I think the suggestion emanated from Prof. Bremner. I mentioned it to my brother who readily agreed to send me to Cambridge to take my degree in Philosophy. I went to England in the following month. To my great surprise I found that the University would not permit me to appear for the degree examination until I had passed the previous examination of that University, which included among other subjects familiar to me, Latin with which I was wholly unacquainted. I however managed to study enough of it to be able to pass that examination which I did in the following October. I attended the lectures in Economics and History of such distinguished men as Prof. Henry Sidgwick, Mr. Alfred Marshall and Sir John Seely. Dr. Keynes taught me Economics. They all agreed that my knowledge of these subjects was sufficiently advanced to permit of my going up for the degree examination in the following June ; but the rules of the University were inflexible. They required that only students who had attended lectures for seven terms and put in residence of two years could appear for the honours examination of the University. Prof. Henry Sidgwick moved the University to relax the rules in my favour. He told me that I had received such good training in India that I knew all the subjects connected with the Moral Philosophy honours examination and that I should be wasting my time studying the same subjects over again at Cambridge. All these are compliments not to me but to my professor, Mr. Bremner, who had interested himself in my education and had put into me all that was best in him on these subjects. I told Prof. Henry Sidgwick of what I owed to Prof. Bremner, and he was surprised that in India one could get such good teaching. To see whether I had merely memorised or assimilated the subjects in which I professed student who was qualifying for Honours, it was more coaching than teaching me. Further the class consisted of one and it met in a small partitioned room screened off from the main hall by a canvas partition which ran along the whole width of the hall, sub-dividing the portion into three small compartments. Of these one was used as the Professor's retiring room, the central one as the B. A. (Hon.) class-room, and on the other end, the partitioned room contained 3 or 4 almirahs of very ancient books. It was the established rule of the college that the first half-hour should be devoted to the teaching of the Bible. This practice continued even after the old Free Church Institution had ceased to exist. Prof. Bremner used to teach the combined classes the Holy Scripture. He found the students somewhat impatient with his teaching of the Bible, and he introduced a variety in the Scripture-teaching by announcing that he would take during Bible hour Prof. Drummond's book on spiritual law in the physical world. This was a welcome change to many students to whom the novelty of the subject was highly attractive. The class became packed with eager students and the lectures used to be heard with increasing attention. The half hour assigned to the lecture was found too short and sometimes a few extra minutes had to be devoted to the completion of the day's lecture. It was not long before Prof. Bremner had endeared himself to the students. Almost from the first the students took kindly to him. His appearance was kind, his manner gentle and his treatment of his students most friendly and sympathetic. He was master of the subject he was called upon to teach the students and he felt at home whether he was teaching Mathematics, History, English or Philosophy. The B.A. Honours course in English and Philosophy in those days was tough, —I dare say it is tougher now. The number of books one had to study ran into a score or more. Uberweg's History of Philosophy had to be got through as a part of the Honours course of the day. Kant's Criticism of Reason was naturally the very bite for an Honours student. The fact is that the Calcutta University prescribed all the known books in Philosophy for their B. A. Honours students, but in assigning marks the examiners who were appointed from Calcutta gave preference to the books which they themselves had taught to

Of the two professors who impressed me greatly during my college-days, one was Prof. Bremner and the other was my old friend Lala Bhagirat Prashad. I can never forget the magnetic personality of both these professors. The college-boys swore by them. They were their pet Professors, and they often played pranks upon them to show that they loved them. I shall mention one incident which occurred within my own personal knowledge. As stated before we had a large combined class to which Prof. Bremner used to lecture, during the first half hour, on a sacred subject. My old friend Mr. Dhundi was a student of this class at the time. His mechanical brain had already been stimulated and he used to take up the boys' watches, time-pieces, etc. for mending. As such he brought back to the college a highly sonorous alarm time-piece after repairing it for a student. We had a look at it, and it happened that the alarm was wound up just five minutes before the half-hour was to be over. The student had placed his cleaned clock safely in his pocket. Puntually to the minute the time-piece sounded the alarm and set the whole class alaughing. But the poor dumb-founded student from whose pocket the wierd noise rang out was kept in wonder and asked the clock to be quite. All that he could ejaculate was "Chop" "Chop." He did not know how it all happened, though he accused me of being the last person to have touched the time-piece. This became a standing college-joke and amused the students for a long time and I hope that Mr. Dhundi did not on that account lose his other customers.

The Hislop College had a serious rival in the Morris College which had just then been started. Its Principal was Dr. Stanley Shaw who hailed from Dublin. The college used to meet in a small building in Tulsi Bagh. In order to establish a friendly relationship between the students of the two colleges, Mr. Fraser, afterwards, Sir Alexander Fraser suggested the idea of starting an inter-collegiate debating society. The inaugural meeting was held at which Mr. Fraser unfolded his scheme which was loudly applauded. The Inter-collegiate debating society was set on foot, and its meetings used to take place on Saturday afternoons at 2. Prof. Bremner was appointed its permanent President and though he spoke but little at the meetings, the success of the society was largely due to his efforts.

to be acquainted, he questioned me closely and being satisfied of my attainments recommended the passing of a special statute exempting me from the ordinary rules of residence and seniority. The subsequent examination to which I was admitted justified his anticipations. Then I wrote to Mr. Bremner thanking him for what he had taught me and of the excellent result I had shown at the honours examination of the University—an examination, by the way, which is up to this day regarded with holy horror by the students of the University and for which no more than half the students used to compete every year. Though owing to Prof. Bremner's excellent teaching I had passed my Moral Science Tripos, I was soon confronted with a difficulty, but as it is not connected with Prof. Bremner I shall pass it over.

While at Cambridge I was in regular correspondence with Prof. Bremner who used to assist me in my studies by making valuable suggestions. I wrote a volume of verse which I sent to him for criticism and it greatly helped me in composing my next volume which had a fairly large vogue in the University circles. I competed for the Chancellor's medal in English verse and before submitting my thesis I sent it to Prof. Bremner for criticism and I well remember his words in which he counselled me not to devote more than my ordinary leisure for the composition of verse.

On my return to this country in 1892 I paid a visit to my old college and saw Mr. Whitton, but to my great surprise I afterwards learnt that Prof. Bremner had left the college for good. However, I was very glad to welcome him upon his rejoining the college. Some ten years back, when he and I used to frequently exchange visits and on one of these occasions I remember Prof. Bremner being offered a responsible appointment in a University just then started. But Prof. Bremner with his usual modesty said that he was too old to accept the job. That was four years ago. I still feel that the University has seriously lost by his non-acceptance of the offer. He would have been an ornament to that University as he was an ornament to the Hislop College. My college life with Prof. Bremner was the college life more akin to that to which I became subsequently acquainted in England.

IN MANCHURIA

MANCHURIA can be described as India under British rule, and the Japanese have followed the British model of colonial expansion and administration, the only difference being that the British model is more subtle : it is more thorough-going than the Japanese. I would much rather be a slave of Japan than the slave of England, if I have to be a slave at all. The people in Manchuria cannot construct a factory, or manufacture goods without a license and this license is only given to the Japanese or to companies with dominant Japanese interests. The people are disarmed and the bulk of them have taken to smoking opium and eating it, which, in fairness to Japan, it must be said, was their failing under the Chinese regime, which the Japanese have not eliminated but regulated and controlled, as the British have done in this country.

I went into the interior of Manchuria and found life static, primitive and indescribably filthy except in tourist-centres, where the Japanese took foreigners on their personally conducted tours. I had three interpreters with me ; an American missionary, a Korean graduate of an American University, and a Japanese attache. I found that the Japanese kicked and knocked down the Manchurian as the tommy did punkha-coolie in India, and the Manchurian took it for granted that these kicks were meant for the conqueror's kisses. For he did not resent them. If a coolie was late in following me with the luggage from the station, the Japanese never spoke to him but merely went and kicked him, and it had the desired effect, though in stature a Manchurian is a giant as compared to a Japanese ; the average height of the Manchurian being about 5 feet 8 inches and of Japanese, 4 feet 2 inches.

I was very grieved to see a fine University building constructed by a Chinese Governor out of his ill-gotten gains, deserted, and in charge of the Japanese sentry. I took permission to walk through it. It was a perfectly designed University, three miles long and about two miles wide, with its spacious hostels, lecture-rooms, laboratories and common rooms. The University had 4,000 students before

I fear my reminiscences have already outrun the space allotted to me. I must therefore bring them to an abrupt termination. I shall only add, before concluding, that of all the professors I have met I have never loved one as I loved Prof. Bremner. He was the noblest, the kindest and the best of all the professors that it was my privilege to come across. I shall be glad if the college will commemorate his association with it by some enduring monument.*

*Reprinted from *Hislop College Magazine.*

with first class foreign food (American dishes and orthodox 'Home food', *i.e.*, Japanese dishes). The cost is reasonable and not prohibitive. The servants bring you the hot water with towels to wash your face and hand, to wipe out the dust and smoke of the train. But there is no dust or smoke in the trains, as most of them are lined on a first class bunker-coal or electricity.

The Japanese sense of cleanliness clings to the people wherever they go. I found, however, a strange contrast between the amenities of the Japanese railway system and those of Manchuria. In Japan, no one dared enter a higher class compartment without authority. In Manchuria, no one dared turn out the crowds of military, who trooped into the first class and higher class compartments where they made themselves thoroughly at home ; with the result that the first class was as often as not as crowded, if not more crowded, as the third class. This absolute lack of check and discipline among passengers is hard to explain. But on closer observation, I found that the intruders in the higher classes were all Japanese, who felt free to travel in any class with or without tickets. This was explained to me by a Korean guide, who prided himself upon the fact that it was one country where travelling was free ! *

*Reprinted from *'Facts and Fancies'*.

the Japanese occupation. I could get no information as to why the University had closed down. But I really needed no information on the subject, as the Japanese believe that "ignorance is the ally of servitude" and that if you wish to keep the people down, you must keep them ignorant so that their consciousness and self-respect remain dormant.

I went to Harbin and from there to a large city on the verge of Siberia, where I found a large Asiatic colony. In the whole of Manchuria, as in India, the town consists of various sections, situate far apart, like the Indian cities where the civil stations are separate from the town by a belt of sanitary zone. Such was the case in Manchuria. The Japanese town was scrupulously clean, well-laid out and perfectly safe at night. The Russian colony was the same ; but, perhaps, not so safe as the Japanese zone. I met a large number of Russian women, serving as waitresses in the restaurants. They said that they belonged to White Russia and wanted to come to India as they had heard a lot about her ; but the fact is that every Russian who immigrates across Siberia, calls himself White Russian to prevent the odium of being classed as a Soviet Russian, against which there was as much prejudice in Japan as in Manchuria.

There were a few newspapers in Manchuria and I used to get them every morning. They were the dullest papers I have ever read. They translated in Chinese the official and semi-official news from the Japanese papers. From Manchuria to Pekin, there is a fine railway. But under the Chinese regime, it was frequented by bandits, who used to rob travellers, and used fire-arms for robbing them. The Japanese have cleared the bandits from the whole of this land by making the adjoining villages collectively responsible for the safety of life, an arrangement, like that of which obtains on the Peshawar-Jalalabad roadway.

All the trains in Manchuria are built and run on the American lines. The first class passenger trains are beautifully furnished with easy chairs, opening on all the windows, and a conductor acts as a waiter to the passengers, who can obtain their steno-typists, as they get along in the train. They have their own writing-rooms, Posts, Telephones and Telegrams ; while the dining rooms are replete

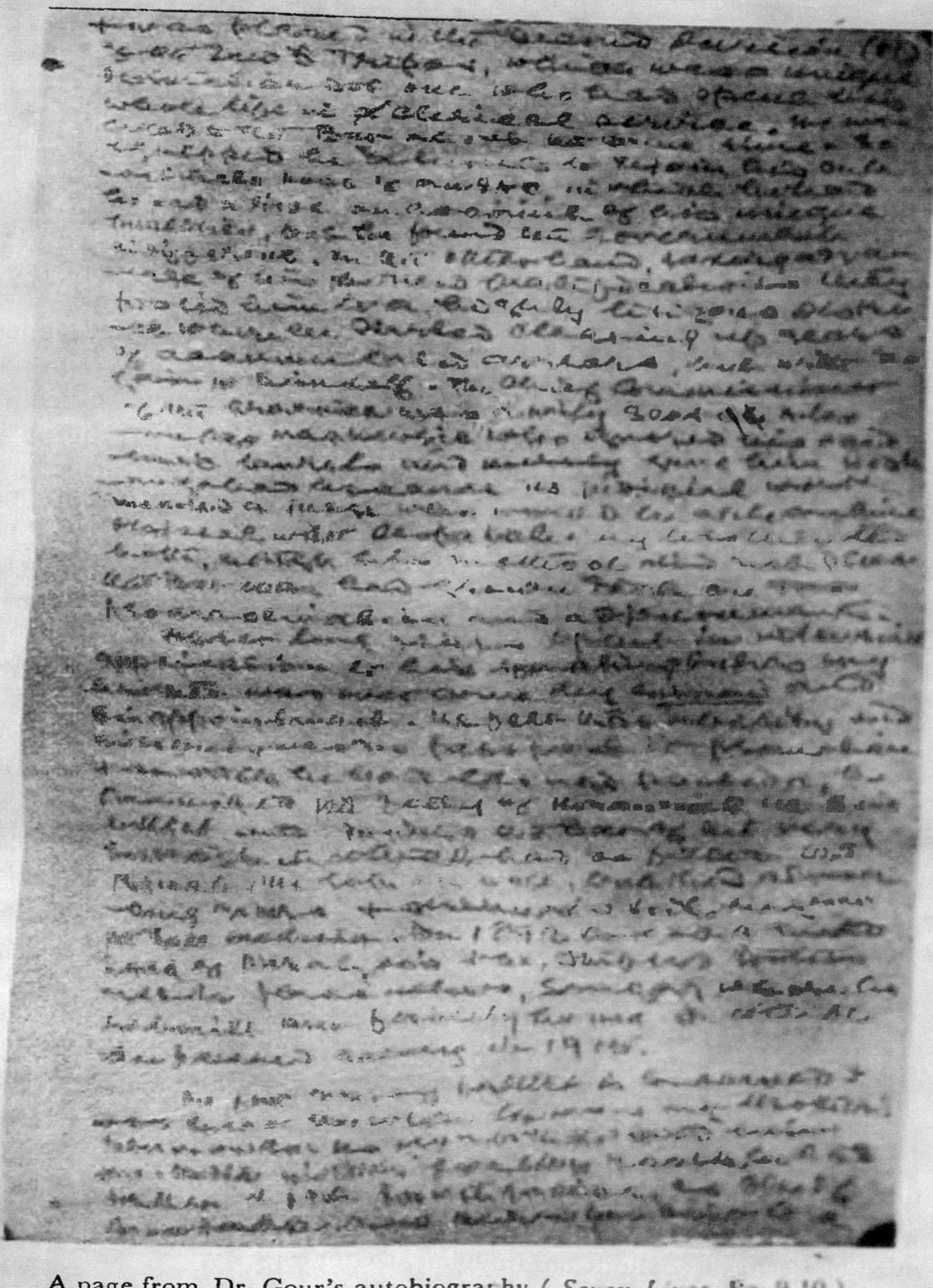

A page from Dr. Gour's autobiography (*Seven Lives*, Pp. 9-10)

MY WORLD TOUR

CHARACTER in all walks and stations of life may be displayed in all spheres of human action. There is the historic fact of Socrates who was condemned to death by the poisonous cup of Hemlock. He had a chance of escape and his friends advised him to do so. But he refused. He said he had been condemned to death and he would not evade the law. He quietly took the poison and died. He was a hero and there are thousands of other cases where people have ungrudgingly yielded to the call of duty. That duty may be the command of a righteous or a tyrannical sovereign, but the man of character obeys it, though the man of a different character would rise against it even though he may be shot for it. Character therefore does not imply identical action in all cases, but what it does imply is courage and virtue which heightens and ennobles mankind.

A man may show his character, integrity, honesty and straightforward conduct in any branch of life. A man who sells his goods and advertises for sale is justly treated as dishonest if he puffs them up as possessing the imaginary quality which he knows they do not possess and he passes them on as genuine when they are to his knowledge counterfeit. Such dishonesty in trade is universal or confined to a large class of men, which does not in the slightest degree contest dishonesty. On the other hand, it condemns not only the man but the community or class to which he belongs. A man may by his strenuous work invent or perfect an invention. Another man copies it and uses it for his profit. All reasonable men would treat this as arrant deception and fraud, but there are communities and persons who regard it as a sign of cleverness. It is reported that the Greeks who were extremely clever but not equally honest ridiculed the Romans if they paid their debts when they were barred by time. In the best days of the Roman Republic, honesty was their national trait and the Greek Republic fell, because of their over-cleverness without commensurate honesty.

In my world tour, I can bear witness to the following instances I personally saw and which make their own comments on the national character of a new country like Japan and countries like France, England and America.

When I was in Japan, I toured all over the country and in one Hotel, far away from everywhere, I stayed at night with my daughter Rubie (now Mrs. Rubie Sulochana Nanda) who was my never-failing companion in my world tours. In the morning I had to leave to deliver a lecture in a place three miles from the Hotel. On my return my daughter wanted to make some purchases and wanted me to pay for them. I then found that I had left behind my money bag under my pillow. I told my secretary and he said, "It does not matter ; the money can be paid when you return." I returned home and looked for my money bag under the pillow, but it was missing. I rang for Boy San, *i.e.*, the room bearer, and told him so. He immediately took out his key and from a locker produced the bag which was in tact containing money amounting to about £13. I was to have left that Hotel that very evening at 4 o'clock of which Boy San knew.

In England, there is an American firm of Messrs. Woolworth & Co., who have chain shops all over England. They are spacious shops where all kinds of goods are displayed with only a few shop girls. People come and examine the goods and make their selection and pay for them. If they do not, there is, nobody to watch them except a few detectives who are kept to keep an eye on the pilferers.

In France, every morning stacks of newspapers are kept for sale with no one in charge. The money-box is placed alongside and people buy their newspapers and deposit the prices in the box. In America the same system is followed.

In Osaka, I went to see a large number of textile mills, the workers of which have their quarters in long rows, each allotted a room in which there is a wall cupboard, in which the girls keep their clothes, cash and jewellery with no lock on the cupboard. I asked my secretary to open one of them and he did. It contained in the cash-box money amounting to about £3 in value. When I asked the Secretary why the wall almirahs were not locked, he exclaimed why

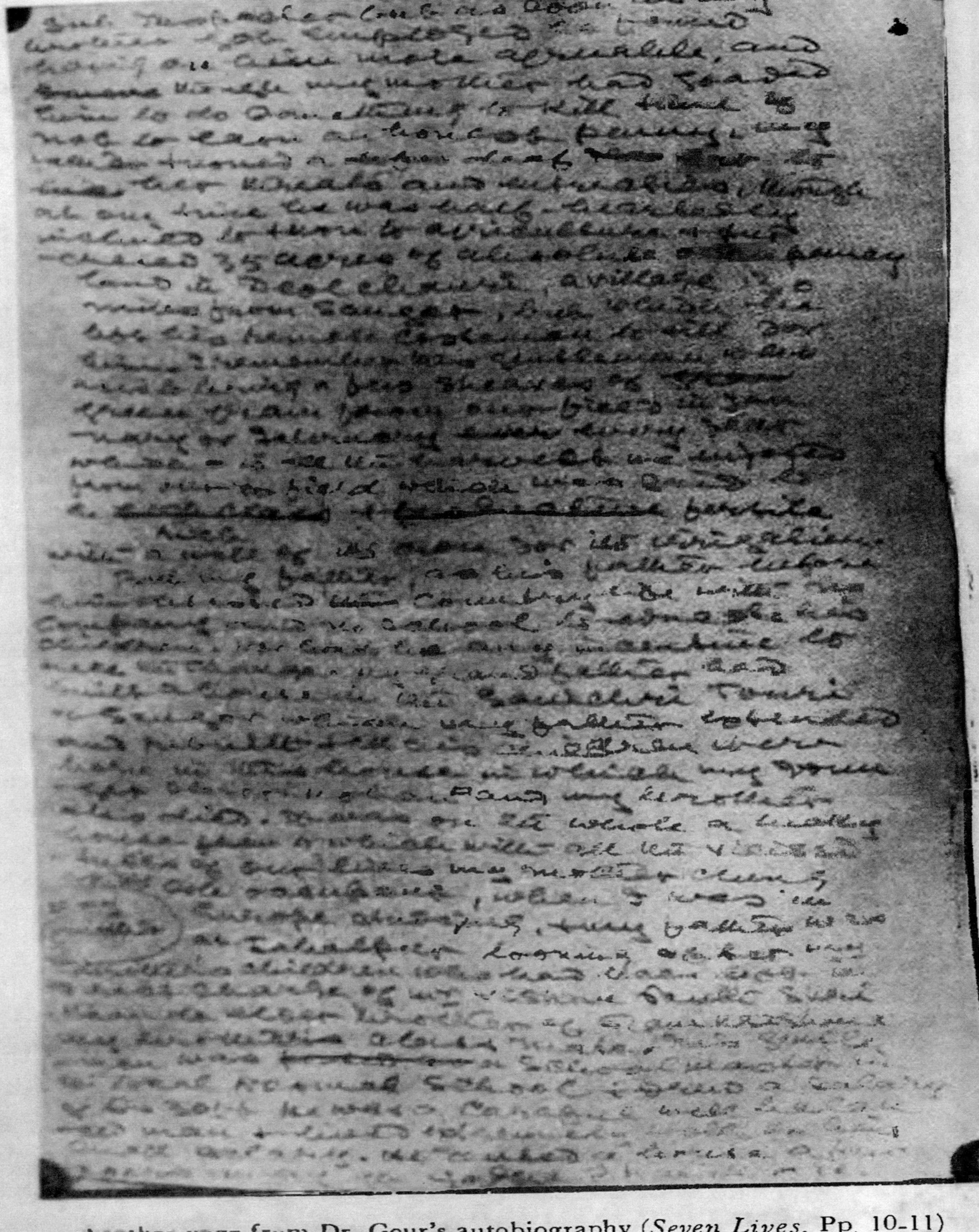

Another page from Dr. Gour's autobiography (*Seven Lives*, Pp. 10-11)

should they be locked. The fact is that hundreds of girls keep their jewellery, cash and clothes in these almirahs and leave them open, but there are no thefts.

About twenty miles from anywhere I went and saw an open air restaurant in which the tables and chairs and drinking cups, knives, forks and other cutlery was exhibited with no one in charge. I asked my secretary the reason. He said the customers would come at 4 in the evening for their tea, but there was no one in charge of the valuable cutlery and other restaurant equipment. These facts surprised me and I asked my Secretary whether there were no thefts. He exclaimed, why should there be ? I reported this instance to the British Ambassador at Tokyo and he confirmed my query stating that the Japanese were scrupulously honest not only to their own people but to all comers. A national character is formed by the people's individual honesty and scrupulousness. It was an eye-opener to me in the light of what I had experienced in my own country.

It is quite true that the Indian character has deteriorated during the last 1500 years of foreign domination, but the only solution is in the establishment of self-government in the country which after long struggle has at last arrived. But the old character of the people continues and will continue till it is reformed by new education and more experience. As it is, a large number of crooks have taken to starting public companies placing at the head of their prospectus the names of prominent men who freely lend their name, and when questioned they confess that they know nothing about the company or its promoter, but have lent their name and when asked why, their simple reply is : What is the harm ? That is the value they place upon their own character. They do not realize what harm they do to the people by their association with such companies. *

* Reprinted from '*Facts and Fancies.*'